UNIVERSITY OF CALGARY
Press

# DOING DEMOCRACY
# DIFFERENTLY

## Indigenous Rights and Representation in Canada and Latin America

# ROBERTA
# RICE

Global Indigenous Issues Series
ISSN 2561-3057 (Print) ISSN 2561-3065 (Online)

University of Calgary Press
2500 University Drive NW
Calgary, Alberta
Canada T2N 1N4
press.ucalgary.ca

LIBRARY AND ARCHIVES CANADA CATALOGUING IN PUBLICATION

Title: Doing democracy differently : Indigenous rights and representation in Canada and Latin America / Roberta Rice.
Names: Rice, Roberta, author.
Series: Global indigenous issues series ; no. 4.
Description: Series statement: Global indigenous issues series ; no. 4 | Includes bibliographical references and index.
Identifiers: Canadiana (print) 20240382838 | Canadiana (ebook) 20240382870 | ISBN 9781773855646 (softcover) | ISBN 9781773855639 (hardcover) | ISBN 9781773855653 (open access PDF) | ISBN 9781773855660 (PDF) | ISBN 9781773855677 (EPUB)
Subjects: LCSH: Indigenous peoples—Canada—Politics and government. | LCSH: Indigenous peoples—Latin America—Politics and government. | LCSH: Indigenous peoples—Canada—Government relations. | LCSH: Indigenous peoples—Latin America—Government relations. | LCSH: Indigenous peoples—Legal status, laws, etc.—Canada. | LCSH: Indigenous peoples—Legal status, laws, etc.—Latin America.
Classification: LCC E98.T77 R53 2024 | DDC 323.1197/071—dc23

The University of Calgary Press acknowledges the support of the Government of Alberta through the Alberta Media Fund for our publications. We acknowledge the financial support of the Government of Canada. We acknowledge the financial support of the Canada Council for the Arts for our publishing program.

Alberta Government | Canadä | Canada Council for the Arts | Conseil des Arts du Canada

Copyediting by Ryan Perks
Cover Image: Colourbox 31613660
Cover design, page design, and typesetting by Melina Cusano

*To Sid and our boys, Ryan and Rhys*

# Contents

Tables and Figures                                                      ix
Abbreviations                                                           xi
Acknowledgements                                                       xiii

INTRODUCTION
Re-envisioning Democracy at the Intersection of                         1
Comparative and Indigenous Political Inquiry

CHAPTER 1
Decolonizing Democracy: Theoretical and Conceptual                     21
Considerations

CHAPTER 2
Yukon: Leading the World in Nation-to-Nation Indigenous                 37
Self-Government

CHAPTER 3
Bolivia: Advancing Indigenous Governance as a Distinct                 53
Order of Government

CHAPTER 4
Nunavut: Enacting Public Government as Indigenous                       71
Self-Government

CHAPTER 5
Ecuador: Promoting Plurinationality through Local                      87
Indigenous Governments

CONCLUSION
Instituting Indigenous and Democratic Governance                      103
Innovations

Notes                                                                 113
References                                                            117
Index                                                                 141

# Tables and Figures

*Tables*

TABLE 0.1.  Selected social and economic indicators                                16

TABLE 1.1.  Models of Indigenous autonomy and self-government                       25

TABLE 2.1.  Allocation of Yukon First Nation settlement land by                     45
            square kilometre under the Umbrella Final Agreement

TABLE 2.2.  Yukon land claim boards                                                 47

TABLE 3.1.  Indigenous legislators in Bolivia (lower and upper houses)              60

TABLE 3.2.  Bolivia's lower house legislative circumscriptions and                  61
            eligibility by department

TABLE 4.1.  Major events in the development of Nunavut                              75

TABLE 4.2.  Nunavut land claim boards                                               83

TABLE 5.1.  Indigenous legislators in Ecuador's National Assembly                   92

TABLE 5.2.  Ecuadorian referendum and popular consultation results                 100

*Figure*

FIGURE 1.1.  Process of democratic decolonization                                   28

# Abbreviations

ADN      Acción Democrática Nacionalista (National Democratic Action)

AIOCs      Autonomías Indígenas Originarias Campesinas (Indigenous First Peoples Peasant Autonomies)

CODENPE      Consejo de Desarrollo de las Nacionalidades y Pueblos del Ecuador (Development Council of the Nationalities and Peoples of Ecuador)

CONAIE      Confederación de Nacionalidades Indígenas del Ecuador (Confederation of Indigenous Nationalities of Ecuador)

COOTAD      Código Orgánico de Organización Territorial, Autonomía y Descentralización (Organic Code of Territorial Organization, Autonomy, and Decentralization)

CTIs      Circunscripciones Territoriales Indígenas (Indigenous Territorial Circumscriptions)

CYFN      Council of Yukon First Nations

CYI      Council for Yukon Indians

DINEIB      Dirección Nacional de Educación Intercultural Bilingüe (National Directorate of Intercultural Bilingual Education)

ECUARUNARI      Ecuador Runacunapac Riccharimui (Awakening of the Indigenous Peoples of Ecuador)

FNFA      First Nation Final Agreement

FPIC      free, prior, and informed consent

IIBA      Inuit Impact and Benefit Agreement

IOL      Inuit Owned Land

IQ      Inuit Qaujimajatuqangit

| | |
|---|---|
| **ITC** | Inuit Tapirisat of Canada |
| **LPP** | Ley de Participación Popular (Law of Popular Participation) |
| **MIP** | Movimiento Indígena Pachakuti (Pachakuti Indigenous Movement) |
| **MIR** | Movimiento de la Izquierda Revolucionaria (Movement of the Revolutionary Left) |
| **MLA** | member of the Legislative Assembly |
| **MNR** | Movimiento Nacional Revolucionario (National Revolutionary Movement) |
| **MUPP** | Movimiento de Unidad Plurinacional Pachakutik (Pachakutik Movement for Plurinational Unity) |
| **NDP** | New Democratic Party |
| **NEP** | New Economic Policy |
| **NIC** | Nunavut Implementation Commission |
| **NLCA** | Nunavut Land Claims Agreement |
| **NTI** | Nunavut Tunngavik Incorporated |
| **NWT** | Northwest Territories |
| **SGA** | Self-Government Agreement |
| **TFN** | Tunngavik Federation of Nunavut |
| **TIPNIS** | Territorio Indígena y Parque Nacional Isiboro-Sécure (Isiboro Sécure Indigenous Territory and National Park) |
| **UFA** | Umbrella Final Agreement |
| **Yasuní-ITT** | Yasuní Ishpingo-Tambococha-Tiputin |

# Acknowledgements

A book such as this one owes a debt of gratitude to many people. As a Canadian academic who studies Indigenous politics in Latin America, one of the first questions I am most often asked by interviewees is, What is it like for Indigenous peoples in Canada? This research project was born out of a commitment to answer that question. In so doing, I learned so much about the country that I call home. I am eternally grateful for this opportunity. Field research in northern Canada is very expensive. This book would not have been possible without the financial support of a Standard Research Grant from the Social Sciences and Humanities Research Council of Canada.

I would like to thank the great folks in Bolivia, Ecuador, Nunavut, and Yukon who shared their valuable time and insights into Indigenous politics with me. Thank you for the wonderful work that you do each and every day to make democracy work for all of us.

A special thanks to Graham White for suggesting the Yukon as a fruitful comparison to Ecuador, and for all the great work that you do on Nunavut. Thanks also go to Kirk Cameron and Ken Coates for introducing me to the wonders of the Yukon!

I would also like to thank Ken Roberts for his ongoing mentorship and conversations on my North-South comparative research design, and Pablo Policzer for his suggestions on the conceptual chapter. Thank you to Allyson Benton for her wonderful idea on how to conceptualize the book in terms of democratic decolonization (as opposed to simply governance innovation) at the 2020 American Political Science Association conference. And thank you to Christopher Carter for organizing that excellent panel and for including me in it!

Last, but not least, a special thanks to the amazing people at the University of Calgary Press for making this book a reality, and to the anonymous reviewers for their helpful comments and suggestions. Any shortcomings remain my own.

I dedicate the book to my husband, Sid, for always supporting my career and being the great father and friend that he is—and to our amazing sons,

Ryan and Rhys, who had to endure my many absences when they were little so that I could carry out the field research for this study. I will never forget the time that I received a late-night phone call while in Whitehorse from my oldest son, Ryan, who had just lost his first tooth at home in Toronto. And I missed it. I can only hope that this book, and the ideas of inclusive change that it carries, are worth it. I love you guys.

# INTRODUCTION

# Re-envisioning Democracy at the Intersection of Comparative and Indigenous Political Inquiry

"We do government differently."[1] This description of territorial politics by an Indigenous member of the Yukon Legislative Assembly, Kevin Barr, of the centre-left New Democratic Party is what initially inspired this book project. The idea of striving "to do government differently" was repeated to me in Nunavut by John Quirke, the clerk of the Legislative Assembly of Nunavut.[2] During a research trip to Bolivia, Félix Cárdenas, the vice minister of decolonization, spoke with me about his government's plans to decolonize and de-patriarchalize Bolivian democracy and the state.[3] And in Ecuador, the national coordinator of the Indigenous-led Pachakutik Movement for Plurinational Unity, Rafael Antuni, outlined for me that party's plans to direct the country's constitutionally recognized plurinational state so as to make democracy work for all citizens.[4] Across the Americas, Indigenous peoples are busy playing a dual political role building up the structures of self-government within their nations while participating in the electoral politics that characterize these settler states. This book tells the story of four successful examples from Canada and Latin America of how to advance Indigenous autonomy and self-determination through existing democratic mechanisms.

Indigenous peoples are increasingly important social and political actors in contemporary democracies worldwide. While much has been written by and about Indigenous peoples in both North and South America, there are few, if any, cross-regional comparative analyses of the tensions and connections between Indigenous groups and the state.[5] This book intends to fill this gap. Indigenous political mobilization in the Americas raises important normative and empirical questions for scholars of comparative politics, democratic theory, and Indigenous studies: Are Indigenous-state relations improving in the region? How are different states responding to Indigenous demands for greater recognition and representation? What are the democratic implications of Indigenous demands for autonomy from the state? In what ways does the project of decolonization unsettle the practice of democracy? These questions are at the heart of this book.

The central objective of the following chapters is to explain how democratic decolonization is being instituted in four different polities, those of Bolivia, Ecuador, Nunavut, and Yukon. The comparison between Canada and Latin America provides analytical leverage for identifying factors that produce distinctive patterns of Indigenous-state relations, with concomitant consequences for the practice of democracy. The book seeks to provide a comparative analysis of democratic innovations in the area of Indigenous rights and representation. It is also meant to contribute to the imaginative and practical task of exploring what democracy could mean and become beyond the "straitjacket of state politics" (Picq 2017, 2). Based on a structured, focused comparison of these four different cases, the study argues that the capacity for democratic innovation lies within the realm of civil society, while the possibility for the uptake of such innovations is found within the state and its willingness to work with Indigenous and popular-sector actors.

The study's organizational framework is based on Abele and Prince's (2006) quadripartite typology of self-government models. The theoretical approach elaborated below integrates considerations of structure, agency, and institutions. I borrow from the sub-field of comparative politics its logic of comparative inquiry, its attention to issues of conceptual stretching, and its focus on institutions, states, and regimes (Collier and Mahon 1993; George and Bennett 2005; Kohli et al. 1996). From the sub-field of Indigenous politics, I draw on its grounded approach to theory, its emphasis on local histories, practices and contexts, and its fundamental notions of resurgence, decolonization, and land-based politics (Asch, Borrows, and Tully 2018; Brooks, Ngwane, and Runciman 2020; Tuck and Wang 2012; Wildcat et al. 2014). Only by operating at the intersection of these two sub-fields of political science is it possible to make meaningful, cross-case comparisons that take seriously the role of institutions and the land on which they are built in bringing about democratic transformation in the Americas. Given the scope of this task, the study largely adopts a macro-institutional approach to the study of self-government. By examining various pathways to democratic decolonization, my goal is not to create a new subtype of democracy (e.g., decolonized democracy), but rather to draw out generalizable lessons from real-world examples of how to upend colonial mindsets and practices within existing democracies. Similar to deepening democracy by ensuring more citizen input and control, democratic decolonization is a process, not a regime type (Roberts 1998). A central premise of the book is that liberal democracy is not the end point of democratic development. In order to do democracy better, and not just differently, Indigenous peoples and settler states and societies in Canada and Latin America will need to come to terms with the responsibilities and obligations of having different nations occupying the same space (Ladner 2018).

## Comparative Indigenous Politics

Indigenous politics has long been invisible to political science (Falleti 2021). Ferguson (2006) goes a step further with his provocatively titled article "Why Does Political Science Hate American Indians?" He argues that the discipline is so structured around the state as the primary unit of analysis, including in its technical questions of comparative method and statistical analysis, that non-state actors, even those with sovereign power such as Indigenous peoples, disappear from scholarly view (1031). Much of the concern in the literature has been with formal institutions and how to strengthen them (e.g., Brinks, Levitsky, and Murillo 2020; Huntington 1972; Mainwaring and Scully 1995). At the risk of stating the obvious, formal institutions are institutions of the state. In the Americas, state institutions have been imposed upon pre-existing Indigenous nations. Such institutions have not historically served the interests of Indigenous peoples well (Eversole 2010). According to Barker (2012, 332), "The goal is not to reform imposed systems such that Indigenous peoples can equally benefit from them, but rather to fundamentally decolonize power and place through a transformation of how people relate to and in place." As noted by de Sousa Santos (2009), never before has there been such a great distance between political theory and political practice. Instead of studying what social actors *should* be doing, we should study what they *are* doing. In places such as northern Canada and the central Andes, Indigenous peoples are remaking democracy to serve their needs and interests, and in so doing they are working to improve the quality of democracy in highly exclusionary societies. Deeper dialogue between democratic theorists and scholars of Indigenous politics would help to close the gap between conceptions of democracy from above and the ideas and practices of democracy from below (Brooks, Ngwane, and Runciman 2020).

Why compare Indigenous rights and representation in Canada and Latin America? There are tremendous differences between both places in terms of levels of economic development, political culture, state capacity, and institutional arrangements. Yet, in both regions, Indigenous peoples have been working to transform a historic relationship with the state that has been characterized by domination and marginalization into one based on mutual respect and understanding and in which all parties are able to pursue their economic, social, and political interests (Altamirano-Jiménez 2013; González et al. 2021; Lindau and Cook 2000). Comparative Indigenous scholarship is needed to provide a better understanding of how Indigenous peoples navigate between Indigenous and settler worlds beyond the established democracies of Canada, the United States, Australia, and New Zealand (e.g., Maaka and Fleras 2005; Scholz 2006; Simpson 2014). According to Kuokkanen (2019, 7), "In order to comprehend and appreciate the complexity and diversity of Indigenous political autonomy and self-determination, it is necessary to transcend discourses, approaches and models created in the Anglo-settler democracies." There is no one, single way to decolonize democracy. Instead, there are multiple responses, pathways, and possibilities to decolonize states and democracies. In the words of Skocpol (cited in Kohli et al. 1995, 45), "it pays to compare."

One of the ways in which comparative Indigenous political inquiry has paid off has been in offering new insights into the structuring principle of settler colonialism in the Americas. Settler colonialism is a particular form of structured domination in which groups of people (settlers) leave their countries to establish a permanent homeland elsewhere by way of the displacement of others (Veracini 2016; Wolfe 1999). Premised on the acquisition of land, settler colonialism not only dispossesses Indigenous peoples of their territories and self-determining authority, but also impedes the transmission of knowledge about forms of governance that arise from Indigenous people's relationships with and on the land (Coulthard 2014; Singh 2019; Wildcat et al. 2014). Settler colonial theory, which considers settler colonialism to be a feature principally of British imperialism, is rarely applied to Latin America (Castellanos 2017; Martínez 2016). Instead, Spanish and Portuguese imperial projects, which are suggested to be rooted in labour rather than land expropriation, are characterized as forms of extractive colonialism (Altamirano-Jiménez 2013). Speed (2017), whose work questions this land-labour divide, argues that in Latin America, Indigenous peoples were subjected to both land dispossession and labour extraction. She laments the artificial divide between the Global North and Global South in Indigenous studies scholarship and finds that there is a dual theoretical gap in the literature, writing that "theorizations of the settler state (largely elaborated in the north) have not grappled fully enough with neoliberal capitalism, and theories of the neoliberal state (a primary focus in the south) fail to recognize the significance of settler logics that structure the conditions of state formation, including in its current iteration" (784). Likewise, Gott (2007) proposes that we resist viewing Latin America as a continent conveniently set apart from the general history of European settler colonialism in the Americas. In this vein, the unfolding of Indigenous politics in Canada and Latin America provides excellent fodder for comparative analysis.

Colonial history structures Indigenous-state relations within a country, which in turn condition the possibilities and pathways for decolonizing institutions, states, and regimes. European colonization in the Americas, despite a number of common features, resulted in the creation of different economies and polities owing to the encounters between distinct European countries and differing local environments (Lindau and Cook 2000). There are marked differences between Indigenous-state relations in Canada and Latin America. For instance, the Canadian state has traditionally assumed an interventionist role with regard to Indigenous peoples, such as in determining who is and who is not Indigenous and in designing band council governments and outlining internal election procedures (Belanger 2008; Lindau and Cook 2000; Maaka and Fleras 2005). In contrast, Latin American states have generally either disregarded Indigenous peoples, whose communities remained largely beyond the reach of the state, or attempted to recast them as peasants and workers (Rice 2012; Stavenhagen 2002; Yashar 2005). Nevertheless, as revealed by the broad contours of Indigenous-state relations in Canada and Latin America outlined in the next section, states in both regions have worked to dispossess Indigenous peoples of their lands and livelihoods, divide them, categorize them in ways that obscure their identity, discount them from national policy debates, and denigrate them as obstacles to economic growth and development. Viewed through a comparative Indigenous politics lens, states in Canada and Latin America have an uncanny resemblance.

## Indigenous-State Relations in Canada

Section 35 of Canada's Constitution Act, 1982, identifies Indigenous peoples as First Nations (i.e., "status Indians"), Inuit, and Métis. Indigenous peoples account for almost 5 per cent of the total population in Canada. Subsumed within these legislated categories are approximately forty to sixty distinct nations or peoples (Abele and Prince 2006). Indigenous-state relations in Canada have been governed by the Royal Proclamation of 1763, the British North America Act of 1867, the Indian Act of 1876, and the pre- and post-Confederation treaties (McNeil 2001; Tully 1995; Turner 2006). The Royal Proclamation of 1763, which claimed British royal sovereignty over Indigenous peoples, set out the rules regarding the treatment of Indigenous peoples and their lands. Following Confederation in 1867, a process by which the Dominion of Canada came into being as a united federation, section 91 of the British North America Act (later renamed the Constitution Act, 1867) gave the federal government of Canada legislative authority over Indigenous peoples (Lindau and Cook 2000). Canada's Constitution Act, 1867, provides the legal authority for the much-reviled Indian Act of 1876, the main legislative basis for the country's Indigenous policy.

The Indian Act continues to serve as the key mechanism of federal policy over First Nation communities. It has allowed the federal government to intervene in the daily affairs of Indigenous peoples to an extent unparalleled in the Americas (Maaka and Fleras 2005). The act defines who is a "status Indian" for government administrative and entitlement purposes. Status is conferred on Indigenous people who are signatories or descendants of signatories to a treaty or party to some other exceptional administrative arrangement with the Canadian government (Lindau and Cook 2000; Tully 2000). Legal status provides First Nations people with special rights and benefits, including the right to live on reserve lands, limited tax exemptions, and certain health and education benefits. Many Indigenous people do not have status. Federal policy denies any special rights to non-status Indigenous people (Abele and Prince 2006; Papillon 2008). Up until 1985, with the passage of Bill C-31 ("A Bill to Amend the Indian Act"), First Nations women who married non-Indigenous men automatically lost their status under the provisions of the Indian Act (Brown 2003). Palmater (2011) has suggested that Canada's system of legislated Indigenous identity serves the state's agenda to control, divide, and assimilate Indigenous peoples. As Duncan Campbell

Scott, Canada's deputy superintendent of Indian and northern affairs from 1913 to 1932, infamously wrote, "Our objective is to continue until there is not a single Indian in Canada that has not been absorbed into the body politic and there is no Indian question" (cited in Palmater 2011, 28). Regarded as wards of the state, First Nations people were denied the right to vote in federal elections until 1960 (Milen 1991).

The treaty relationship between Indigenous peoples and the state is one that sets Canada apart from Latin America. Treaties recognize both parties as equal, coexisting, and self-governing (Tully 2000). Historically, the government signed treaties with Indigenous peoples to legally secure land for settlement. Treaties also served to legitimate the settler state's presence on Indigenous lands (Starblanket 2020). Between 1701 and 1921, more than seventy treaties were signed between leaders of Indigenous nations and representatives of the British Crown (Belanger 2014, 78). Prior to Confederation, treaties served a mainly strategic purpose, while the post-Confederation treaties, including the "numbered treaties" across much of the West, were meant to advance the country's economic development (Lindau and Cook 2000, 9). The treaties contained an extinguishment clause, under which the various implicated Indigenous peoples were required to relinquish all existing and possibly existing land rights to vast territories in exchange for reserve lands, goods, and services (Blackburn 2007; Maaka and Fleras 2005). Canada's unusual land-settlement process has been the subject of criticism both domestically and internationally, including from the United Nations (Rice 2014b). The trajectory in the relationship between Indigenous peoples and the state in Canada is one in which the original treaty-based relationship was eventually replaced by policies aimed at displacing Indigenous people so as to facilitate further settlement and then, later, assimilating Indigenous people into the dominant society (Tully 2000).

Until the 1960s and the rise of the contemporary Indigenous rights movement, Canada's policy toward Indigenous peoples was based on assimilationist goals: conversion to Christianity; establishment of the reservation system; subjugation of Indigenous culture through residential schools; and imposition of Western-style band council governments (Lindau and Cook 2000). The release of the *Final Report of the Truth and Reconciliation Commission* of Canada in June 2015 is seen by some observers as a critical moment in Canadian history. The TRC was established as a condition of the 2006 Indian Residential Schools Settlement Agreement between the Canadian government and the approximately 86,000 living survivors of residential schools (Corntassel and Holder 2008). The federal government's involvement in residential schools began in earnest in the 1880s when it took a more active role in the development and administration of the schools in partnership with the churches. In 1920, the Indian Act was amended to allow the Department of Indian Affairs to compel children to attend residential schools (Regan 2010). During this period, children as young as four were forcibly taken from their homes and brought to residential schools, where their hair was cut and where they were compelled to exchange traditional clothing for uniforms, forbidden to speak Indigenous languages, and were forced to endure physical punishment, and in some cases sexually abused, in what was tantamount to a system of institutionalized child neglect (Helwig 2017). For over a century, the residential school system separated more than 150,000 Indigenous children from their families based on the assumption that Indigenous cultures and spiritual beliefs were inferior, and as a means "to kill the Indian in the child" (TRC 2015, 130). The last residential school closed in Canada in 1996, though most began closing their doors in the 1960s in the face of mounting political pressure.

Paradoxically, the federal government's attempt to terminate its special relationship with Indigenous peoples in the late 1960s stimulated Indigenous political mobilization in the country. The White Paper of 1969 put forward by the minister of Indian affairs sought to abolish the Indian Act, dismantle the Department of Indian Affairs, and eventually eliminate treaty privileges and special status in an attempt to absorb Indigenous peoples into Canadian society (Ladner and Orsini 2003; Lindau and Cook 2000). According to Turner (2006, 13), the backlash generated by the proposal galvanized a new generation of Indigenous leaders to press for greater recognition of Indigenous rights. It also propelled Canada's five main national Indigenous organizations onto the front lines of Indigenous politics—the Assembly of First Nations, the Congress of Aboriginal Peoples, the Inuit Tapiriiksat Kanatami, the Métis National Council, and the Native Women's Association of Canada. There is no overarching organization to unite the diverse array of Indigenous groups and their interests in Canada.

Indigenous peoples have generally used the courts and the language of rights to assert their claims. Canada's long-standing tradition of providing government funding for legal advocacy has served as an important support structure for Indigenous legal mobilization (Aks 2004). The courts have thus played a central role in redefining Indigenous-state relations in the country.

Scholtz (2006) has suggested that the combination of Indigenous political mobilization that began in the 1960s alongside landmark court rulings shifted Canada's policy terrain toward negotiation and away from assimilation. Most notably, the 1973 ruling by the Supreme Court of Canada, known as the Calder decision, forced the government to reconceptualize its political relationship with Indigenous peoples as one between sovereign and self-determining peoples or nations as opposed to dependent wards. The decision recognized Indigenous title and implied that other types of rights might also be recognized under the law. The ruling ultimately led to the key revisions in the Constitution Act, 1982, that formally recognized and affirmed Indigenous and treaty rights. It also opened the door to the modern-day treaty process, now referred to as comprehensive land claims agreements.

In 1996, the Canadian government released the massive, five-volume report of the Royal Commission on Aboriginal Peoples. The commission was tasked with investigating and finding ways to improve relations between Indigenous peoples, the Canadian government, and Canadian society as a whole. The commission recommended the pursuit of a series of legislative and policy goals aimed at allowing greater Indigenous control over their own affairs (Borrows 2002). The commission's final report offered a vision of a renewed nation-to-nation relationship based on the inherent rights of Indigenous people to autonomy and self-government. The commission's recommendations required such far-reaching structural reforms on the part of the Canadian government that political leaders immediately rejected its findings (Frideres 2008). Instead, the government has sifted through the hundreds of policy proposals contained within the report and selected the most politically expedient issues to resolve, such as compensation to victims of residential schools. By doing so, the Canadian government has managed to sidestep the fundamental issue of Indigenous sovereignty (Maaka and Fleras 2005).

## Indigenous-State Relations in Latin America

Latin America came into being through Indigenous dispossession. At the time of the European conquest, between 30 and 70 million people inhabited the continent. Possibly half of the Indigenous population died during this period. Disease, displacement, and forced labour took the lives of millions more (Vanden and Prevost 2009). The estimated number of Indigenous people in the region today ranges from 28 to 40 million, divided among some

670 officially recognized nations or peoples (Layton and Patrinos 2006, 25). Indigenous people are a marginalized majority in Bolivia and Guatemala, a substantial portion of the population in Ecuador and Peru, and a significant minority in most other Latin American countries. Indigenous people's interests have long been excluded from Latin American political agendas, that is, until the 1990s, when Indigenous communities began to mobilize on a variety of fronts in defence of their rights. Race, ethnicity, and power continue to overlap in important ways in Latin American societies, contributing to the ongoing marginalization of Indigenous peoples as well as Afro-descendant populations (Wade 2010). Indigenous mobilization, in particular, has begun to challenge the region's exclusionary governing structures and their failure to meaningfully include, represent, and respond to large segments of the population.

The colonial period, which ran from the late fifteenth to the early nineteenth centuries, saw Indigenous lands divided up into large estates, or haciendas, which were awarded to Spanish and Portuguese conquistadors. Many of the conquistadors were the second- or third-born sons of noblemen, and as such were prohibited from inheriting their fathers' lands in their home countries under Latin law as land went to the first-born son (Chasteen 2011). In the New World, however, they were free to acquire vast territories and live as feudal lords. The Indigenous peoples already living on the land instantly became peasants from whom landowners could extract labour under the *encomienda* system, as long as the landowner took responsibility for instructing them in the Spanish language and Catholic faith (Samson and Gigoux 2016). Indigenous communities that were not absorbed into the hacienda system were required by law to pay a head tax or tribute to the state as well as a set amount of free labour to the landowners, the owners of the mines, or the state for public works under the *repartimiento* system. However hated and onerous the institution of the head tax was, it imparted traditional colonial rights and obligations to Indigenous people by virtue of their status as "Indians" under colonial law (Larson 2004). In some countries, the head tax made up more than 50 per cent of public revenues (Platt 1987, 287). This practice lasted well into the independence period as a means to fund the state. In contrast to North America, European settlers in the Spanish and Portuguese Americas did not generally bring with them their wives and children. Instead, the conquistadors turned to Indigenous and enslaved African women as their partners, giving rise to an entirely new population of *mestizos*, or mixed-race people (Lindau and Cook 2000; Martínez 2016). It was within this context that Latin America was first developed.

With one exception, there is no history of treaty relations between Indigenous peoples and the state in Latin America. The Parliament of Quilín, convened in 1641 between Spain and the Mapuche people of present-day Chile, recognized the border of the Biobío River and the independence of Mapuche territory to its south (Bengoa 2000, 37). Chilean independence from Spain in 1810 led to the military defeat of the Mapuche by the Chilean army in 1881; this saw the decimation of the Mapuche population, the expropriation of their lands, and their forced relocation onto dispersed *reducciones*, or reserves, surrounded by Chilean settlements (Saavedra 2002; Schulz 2018). Europeans came to stay in Latin America, just as they did in Canada and the United States. When the Latin American republics achieved their political independence in the early nineteenth century, the *criollo* elites, the descendants of the Spanish and Portuguese ruling classes born in the Americas, became the power holders (Gott 2007; Martínez 2016). Settler colonial logic continues to permeate Latin American state structures and institutions. Political elites in the post-independence period wrestled with the question of what to do about their respective nations' large and unassimilated Indigenous populations, as succinctly summarized by Stavenhagen:

> Latin America's ruling classes, unable to wish Indians away, were quite happy to build nations without Indians, and this they have been trying to do for almost two centuries. To their chagrin, as the new millennium dawns, not only are [I]ndigenous peoples still present—and their numbers are rising—but they are actually challenging the very model of the nation-state that ruling groups have tried so conscientiously to build up. (2002, 28–9)

Indigenous sovereignty, embodied by a treaty relationship, has never been recognized by Latin American states (Lindau and Cook 2000). This is one of the fundamental features that distinguishes Indigenous-state relations in Latin America from those in Canada.

Indigenous-state relations in contemporary Latin America can be characterized by three attempts at state-led Indigenous incorporation: state-sponsored corporatism (lasting from the 1930s to the 1980s); neoliberal multiculturalism (the 1980s to the 1990s); and post-neoliberal plurinationalism

(2000s to the present). National attempts to link long-excluded Indigenous populations to the state have generally followed on the heels of economic disruptions that upset the existing contract between state and society (Drake and Hershberg 2006). The first of these major crises occurred in the 1930s with the Great Depression, the impacts of which were felt worldwide. The second occurred in the 1980s, owing to the international debt crisis. And the third was prompted by the massive tide of protest against neoliberalism in the early 2000s that, in some cases, managed to topple successive national governments (Rice 2012). In all instances, major economic dislocations opened the door to new models of development, growth, distribution, participation, and inclusion in the region.

The crisis of the 1930s led to inward-looking development, redistribution, and import-substitution industrialization as a means to decrease Latin America's economic dependency on global markets. This state-led model of development was accompanied by corporatist measures that offered a degree of popular inclusion in national life, though according to the terms set out by the state (Collier 1995). State-sponsored corporatism was based on the regulation of official channels for demand making. This system promoted assimilation into the dominant *mestizo* culture by reconstituting Indigenous people as national peasants. States did this through agrarian reform. In return for access to land, credit, and services from the state, Indigenous people were obliged to organize and define themselves as peasants (Yashar 2005). But while Indigenous people assumed a peasant status before the state, they continued to practise their cultural ways of knowing and being within their communities.

The 1980s debt crisis, which began in Latin America, led to free market reforms as part of the general shift to the neoliberal economic model. One of the immediate consequences of the adoption of the neoliberal model was the weakening of state corporatist institutions in Latin America (Oxhorn 1998). As a result, the primary mode of interest representation for Indigenous communities was severed. In response to the political and economic exclusion resulting from neoliberalism, Indigenous peoples began to mobilize in the 1990s. The states' response to this mobilization has been neoliberal multiculturalism—the active recognition of a minimal package of cultural rights (e.g., bilingual education, recognition of Indigenous identity) but a rejection of socio-economic and political rights (e.g., land, power, and wealth redistribution). In other words, the multicultural policies that accompanied the market-led development model privileged recognition over redistribution as a means of managing difference (Hale 2000; Postero 2007; Van Cott 2000). Hale (2011) has cautioned that under the neoliberal state, the notion of Indigenous autonomy has been translated into the devolution of limited rights and extensive responsibilities to local communities without the corresponding resources or decision-making powers.

Although state-sponsored corporatism and neoliberal multiculturalism proposed distinct models of state-society relations, both targeted Indigenous people as the problem in need of change. In contrast, the latest bid for Indigenous incorporation is challenging the unidirectional relationship between the state and Indigenous groups. The focus is now on transforming the state to better serve and reflect the interests of society (Rice 2020). Plurinationality seeks to develop a bilateral or nation-to-nation relationship between the state and Indigenous groups. A plurinational state recognizes the plurality of cultural, legal, and political systems that exist within a given nation-state and places them on an equal footing (Becker 2011; Walsh 2009). Plurinationality represents an opportunity for governments in Latin America to reconceptualize their political relationship with Indigenous peoples as sovereign and self-determining peoples or nations. Ecuador and Bolivia are the two countries that have made the most progress in this area (Schilling-Vacaflor and Kuppe 2012). Constitutional reforms in Ecuador (2008) and Bolivia (2009) officially recognized the plurinational character of their nation-states. While the demand for plurinationality may be spreading in Latin America, most governments in the region have a long-standing tradition of centralized authority in which Indigenous sovereignty is viewed as a threat to state unity (Stavenhagen 2002).

## Methods and Cases

This study follows the method of a small-N structured, focused comparison (Collier and Collier 2002; George and Bennett 2005). This methodological approach is "structured" in that I make systematic comparisons of Indigenous rights and representation gains in the cases under consideration; and it is "focused" in that only certain aspects of the cases are examined—most notably, Indigenous-state relations. My comparative cases are Bolivia, Ecuador, Nunavut, and Yukon. This selection of cases was guided by two main criteria. First, despite the vast differences in their social and economic makeup, these polities have witnessed the most successful Indigenous rights movements in the Americas, at least in terms of bringing about institutional change to advance self-determination. The Governments of Bolivia, Ecuador, Nunavut, and Yukon have embarked on ambitious projects of decolonization, albeit to varying degrees, as a result of their engagement with Indigenous movements. Second, the Indigenous movements in these cases are involved in the work of revitalizing Indigenous institutions within their communities while simultaneously engaging with institutions of the settler state. This dual political dynamic is crucial for democratic decolonization, and it may have implications for improving the quality of democracy in cases beyond those under consideration here. My strategy of comparison analyzes similarities and differences among the cases to provide a more nuanced understanding of Indigenous politics. The case studies are presented not with the intention of using them as yardsticks with which to measure one against the other, but rather in the spirit of advancing efforts at democratic decolonization in all of them and providing instructional lessons for Indigenous movements elsewhere that are struggling against colonial-minded governments.

There are political scientists who will object to the comparison of national with sub-national governments in this study, and even those who might balk at the comparison of Canada with Latin America. I take my lead from Canessa (2018) in developing a comparative analysis of Indigeneity. According to Canessa (2018, 209), "As a country with a majoritarian [I]ndigenous discourse, Bolivia has more in common with many African countries than with its Latin American neighbors." Following this logic, it makes little sense to compare Bolivia with Canada as a whole, given that the latter's Indigenous population represents less than 5 per cent of its total population. Yet, Canada is a country of incredible regional variation, ranging from the Indigenous-dominated territories in the North to the settler-dominated provinces in the South, from the large body of French-speakers in the East to the predominantly English-speaking population of the West. When viewed through a sub-national lens, the unique experiments in Indigenous governance in Canada's North call out for comparative analysis. Bolivia and Nunavut are the first large-scale tests of Indigenous governance in the Americas. In both cases, Indigenous people are a marginalized majority who have assumed power by way of democratic mechanisms (see table 0.1). In a broadly similar dynamic, the Governments of Bolivia and Nunavut are working to incorporate Indigenous values, perspectives, and experiences into a liberal democratic order (Anria 2016; Henderson 2009). Ecuador and Yukon also share key features that warrant their comparison, including Indigenous populations that are roughly one-quarter the size of the total populations of each polity and Indigenous movements that have participated in party politics to achieve a modicum of representation within their respective political systems (Alcantara 2013; Rice 2012). A research design based on an innovative approach to comparative case studies is necessary to reveal the rich and complex dynamics that characterize Indigenous politics.

I employ a qualitative research methodology in this study. Qualitative research, which is based on an inductive approach to theory and generalization, is well-suited to exploring and understanding social and political phenomena, especially in unique and deviant cases (Van den Hoonaard 2015). I also draw on principles of Indigenous research methods in my work. Indigenous methodologies contribute to self-determination as defined and controlled by Indigenous communities and as such involve a commitment to respectful relationships with Indigenous peoples and their communities and to doing research by and with, rather than on and for, Indigenous peoples (Kovach 2000; Smith 1999). As a Euro-Canadian settler scholar and ally with graduate degrees in environmental studies and political science from Canadian and US institutions who specializes in Latin American politics and teaches in Indigenous studies and political science programs, I am accustomed to crossing disciplinary, departmental, geographic, cultural, and linguistic divides. There are risks to such academic trespassing. In particular, specialists in Canadian as well as Latin American history and politics will likely disapprove of the cross-regional comparative approach of the book. However, to quote Evans (cited in Kohli et al. 1996, 4) on comparative research, "Neither theories nor cases are sacrosanct." I hope that my search for broader generalizations on Indigenous politics in the Americas generates sufficiently important and interesting questions and insights to warrant the intrusion.

The data for the study were drawn from primary and secondary sources. I carried out four months of field research in Bolivia, Ecuador, Nunavut, and Yukon between June 2012 and August 2014. The study also draws on research material from six months of fieldwork in Bolivia and Ecuador between July 2003 and March 2004 that I conducted as part of my doctoral dissertation. My research findings for the present study are based on personal interviews, primary documents, and secondary sources. I conducted over forty interviews in the four cases with Indigenous leaders, activists, and politicians, government ministers and officials, directors of Indigenous associations, and

**Table 0.1** Selected social and economic indicators (most recent year available)

|  | Bolivia | Ecuador | Nunavut | Yukon |
|---|---|---|---|---|
| Total population size | 11,673,029 | 17,643,054 | 39,536 | 43,118 |
| Total land area (km²) | 1,098,581 | 283,560 | 2,093,190 | 482,443 |
| Indigenous population (%) | 62 | 25 | 84 | 23 |
| Per capita GDP (USD) | 3,143 | 5,969 | 46,981 | 56,931 |
| Mining as % of GDP | 11.0 | 6.0 | 21.1 | 11.1 |
| Infant mortality rate (/1,000) | 35.3 | 16.4 | 21.4 | 5.0 |
| Human Development Index | 0.674 | 0.739 | 0.821 | 0.889 |

*Sources*: Compiled by the author from Economic Commission for Latin America and the Caribbean, Country Profiles (https://estadisticas.cepal.org/); Nunavut Bureau of Statistics (http://www.stats.gov.nu.ca); Statistics Canada (http://www.statcan.gc.ca); United Nations Development Programme (http://hdr.undp.org/); World Atlas (https://www.worldatlas.com/); World Bank (http://data.worldbank.org/); Yukon Bureau of Statistics (https://yukon.ca/en/bureau-of-statistics).

local academics. The interviews were semi-structured and conducted in an interactive, conversational format. The interviewee responses were recorded in a standard notebook. The average interview lasted for thirty minutes. The interviews in Canada were conducted in English, while those in Latin America were done in Spanish. All translations from Spanish to English in this book are my own. I consulted a variety of primary documents in the course of my research, including comprehensive land claims and self-government agreements, constitutions, legislation and laws, government publications, organizational newsletters, and local newspapers. I also relied on the excellent secondary literature produced by area study specialists to strengthen my analysis.

A central claim of this study is that Indigenous-state relations condition the pathway to democratic decolonization. Comprehensive land claims, also known as modern day treaties, in Nunavut and Yukon are a continuation of the historic treaty relationship between Indigenous peoples and the state in Canada. In the absence of treaty relations in Latin America, Indigenous peoples in Bolivia and Ecuador have instead sought constitutional recognition of plurinationality as a means to institutionalize a form of nation-to-nation relationship between Indigenous groups and the state. Strong and well-organized Indigenous movements that have pursued a strategy of institutional engagement have taken the lead in decolonizing efforts in these four cases. Individually, the cases highlight different models and approaches to Indigenous autonomy and self-government that have been achieved in Canada and Latin America. Together, they demonstrate that alternatives to the status quo exist for national as well as sub-national governments.

## The Cases

Yukon is a global leader in modern-day Indigenous self-government. In 1990, the Government of Canada, the Government of Yukon, and what is now the Council of Yukon First Nations signed an Umbrella Final Agreement to establish an innovative model for Indigenous self-government in the territory (Alcantara 2007; Cameron and White 1995). Since then, eleven of the Yukon's fourteen First Nations have successfully negotiated comprehensive land claims and self-government agreements providing them with an impressive array of formal powers, the scope of which are unprecedented in the Americas. The agreements transformed the former Indian Act bands into self-governing First Nations. In terms of territorial rights, self-governing First Nations in the Yukon enjoy surface as well as subsurface rights to much of their settlement lands, including mineral, oil, and gas rights (CYFN and YTG 1997, 11). Self-governing First Nations also have the jurisdictional authority to pass their own constitutions and laws, including the right to determine citizenship and to assume full legislative and delivery responsibilities for their own programs and services if and when they so desire. In matters of general application, First Nations law takes precedence over Yukon law (Cameron and White 1995). In short, the governing power of Yukon First Nations is very much comparable to that of provincial and territorial governments in Canada.

The 1993 Nunavut Land Claims Agreement (NLCA), the largest in Canadian history, brought about substantive change in the governance of the eastern Arctic. In addition to a whole host of land and resource rights, the NLCA resulted in the creation of the new territory of Nunavut. The Inuit-led Nunavut Implementation Commission was tasked with the design and structure of the new government. The Government of Nunavut is modelled largely after the Euro-Canadian parliamentary form of government, with a few key innovations. For instance, the Nunavut Legislative Assembly operates by consensus decision making. There are no political parties in the territory. Instead, candidates run in elections as independents. Most members of the assembly are Inuit and much of the debate is carried out in Inuktitut. Members tend to wear traditional clothing and are seated in a circle, rather than in opposing rows of benches, as in the rest of Canada (White 2006). From the outset, the implementation commission sought to emphasize the distinctiveness of Nunavut. Early goals included incorporating Inuit values and perspectives into the political system, achieving 85 per cent Inuit employment in the new bureaucracy, and having Inuktitut as the working language of the government (NIC 1995; Timpson 2009b). Nunavut's co-management boards dealing with land, wildlife, and environmental issues represent the most significant governance innovation to date. The boards ensure Indigenous participation in policy decisions that are central to Indigenous culture and livelihoods while maintaining federal government control over the use and management of public lands (Nadasdy 2005: Stevenson 2006; White 2008). Nunavut's institutional experiment highlights the centrality of both economic and political rights for advancing Indigenous agendas.

In Bolivia, the 2005 presidential win by Indigenous leader Evo Morales and his Movement toward Socialism party marked a fundamental shift in Indigenous-state relations in the country and in the composition and political orientation of the state. President Morales (who served from 2006 to 2019) made Indigenous rights the cornerstone of his administration in a bid to create a more inclusive polity. The 2009 constitution is central to the advancement of this agenda (Schilling-Vacaflor and Kuppe 2012; Wolff 2012). According to the constitution's preamble, Bolivia has left behind the colonial, republican, and neoliberal state of the past.[6] In its place is a plurinational state that rests on Indigenous autonomy. The new constitution goes further than any previous legislation in the country—and perhaps the world—in securing representation and participation for the nation's Indigenous peoples, including, for example, the recognition of all thirty-six Indigenous languages of Bolivia as official languages of the state (article 5), and the guaranteed right to proportional representation of Indigenous peoples in the national legislature (article 147). It also redefined Bolivian democracy as "intercultural." Intercultural democracy is a hybrid form of democracy that is direct and participatory, representative, and communitarian. Communitarian democracy is based on Indigenous political customs, traditions, and decision-making processes. It is exercised within Indigenous communities through the election or selection of governing authorities. The constitutional recognition of communitarian democracy institutionalizes Indigenous forms of governance as part of the state (Zegada et al. 2011). These, and other such democratic innovations, have made Bolivia's democracy more inclusionary, though decidedly less liberal (Anria 2016).

Ecuador's 2008 constitution was the first in the region to institutionalize Indigenous governing principles as part of the state. Under the direction of the Confederation of Indigenous Nationalities of Ecuador, Ecuador's Indigenous movement was once widely regarded as Latin America's strongest social movement (Van Cott 2005; Yashar 2005). Indigenous mobilization around the enactment of the new constitution resulted in one of the most progressive constitutional texts in the world, both in terms of recognizing the collective rights of Indigenous peoples and in attributing rights to Nature (Caria and Domínguez 2016; Gudynas 2011; Lalander 2014).[7] The new constitution officially proclaimed Ecuador to be a plurinational state, the historic objective of the nation's Indigenous peoples. It also made an explicit commitment to the Indigenous principle of "Living Well" (*Buen Vivir* in Spanish and *Sumac Kawsay* in Kichwa) as an alternative model of development around which the state and its policies are now organized (Bretón, Cortez, and García 2014; Ugalde 2014). The Living Well principle is derived from the Andean Indigenous values of harmony, consensus, and respect, the redistribution of wealth, and the elimination of discrimination, all within a framework that values diversity, community, and the environment (Fischer and Fasol 2013). Although the principle of Living Well presents an opportunity to bring about an alternative to development, it has been used by Ecuadorian governments to justify resource extractivism in the name of progressive social welfare programs (Lalander 2014; Peña y Lillo 2012).

## Plan of the Book

The book is organized into case study chapters that follow the introduction and a first theoretical chapter. Chapter 1 establishes the theoretical and conceptual framework of the study on how to decolonize democracy. It defines and outlines the critical components of a decolonized democratic system. It also highlights the four different models of Indigenous self-government, with varying degrees of autonomy from the state, put forward by Abele and Prince (2006), which are then applied to the book's cases in subsequent chapters.

Chapter 2 examines Indigenous autonomy and self-government in the precedent-setting case of Yukon, Canada. In the Yukon, the successful negotiation of comprehensive land claims and self-government agreements has produced a nation-to-nation relationship between Indigenous peoples and the state on shared land. The objective of this chapter is to explain how Yukon First Nations were able to achieve such a substantial degree of autonomy and self-governing power.

Chapter 3 is devoted to an examination of plurinationality as an exercise of democratic inclusion and power sharing in Bolivia. The chapter is tasked with analyzing the governance innovations of the administration of President Evo Morales, Bolivia's first Indigenous head of state. The inclusion of direct, participatory, and communitarian elements into Bolivian democracy has improved democratic representation for the nation's Indigenous peoples. Nevertheless, serious gaps between legislation and practice still exist.

Chapter 4 is dedicated to a study of Indigenous politics and government in Nunavut. The hopes and aspirations of Inuit hinge on the success of Canada's newest territory. Inuit have opted to pursue self-determination through a public government system rather than through an Inuit-specific self-government arrangement. However, the conditions in which this experiment has thus far taken place are far from ideal. Significant social, economic, and institutional problems plague the new territorial government.

Chapter 5 focuses on the case of Ecuador and the limits to Indigenous autonomy in the face of an intractable government. The populist and left-leaning administration of President Rafael Correa (2007–17) took up most of the political space formerly occupied by Indigenous parties and movements. While the constitutional reform carried out under the Correa administration recognized the plurinational basis of the state, efforts to enact the reforms needed to implement plurinationality have been frustrated by a lack of political will.

The volume ends with a conclusion analyzing the factors that produced distinctive pathways to Indigenous autonomy and self-government in the four cases under consideration. The chapter also explores how participation in institutionalized politics affects Indigenous activism, as well as how activists change institutions and the practice of democracy.

# 1

# Decolonizing Democracy: Theoretical and Conceptual Considerations

The continued exclusion of Indigenous peoples under settler states looms large not only for democratic legitimacy, but also for the quality of democratic institutions and processes (Eversole 2010; Papillon 2008). Democracies in the Americas that operate without Indigenous participation are deficient (CEPAL 2014). Indigenous movements in the cases under consideration in this study see institutional change as key to self-determination. In northern Canada and the central Andes, liberal-inspired democratic orders coexist and compete with traditional and adapted Indigenous governance structures. In between Western and Indigenous forms of governing, however, there exists ample space for political experimentation to link formal with non-formal or non-state institutions as a way to improve overall democratic governability (Retolaza Eguren 2008). To be effective, the process should not formalize all institutions (which would only tilt the political arena to the further advantage of the politically powerful) but should instead promote the productive interplay between both types of institutions. To do so would be to construct a democratic system with the ability to produce the results that civil society demands and to consolidate political institutions that guarantee the inherent rights of Indigenous peoples.

This chapter builds on Abele and Prince's (2006) typology of self-government models in Canada by extending and applying their conceptual framework to Latin America. Despite significant differences in political history and organizational structures among Indigenous nations and peoples in the Americas, it is possible to sort the various forms of self-governing arrangements into models or categories that embody distinct relationships between Indigenous communities and the broader political systems in which they are situated. Each of these models of Indigenous self-government offer differing degrees of autonomy from the state and thus different possibilities and constraints for self-determination. Proceeding from this analytical framework, I establish the criteria for determining the degree of Indigenous autonomy and self-governing power in the book's four case studies. The aim of the chapter is to sharpen our understanding of key theoretical concepts and relationships rather than provide a better specification of measures or indicators of democratic decolonization.

The chapter begins with an overview of the concepts of Indigenous autonomy and self-government in Canada and Latin America as the building blocks for a theory of democratic decolonization. The next section addresses democratic theory as it applies to the institutional experiments that are taking place in northern Canada and the central Andes. The process of democratic decolonization is, as this framework suggests, to be facilitated by an emphasis on governance, as opposed to government, the meaningful inclusion of non-formal institutions into the polity, and the role of citizenship as agency in pushing the boundaries of representative democracy. Special attention is paid in the chapter to how Indigenous institutional participation promotes the growth of new forms of society-centred governance. The chapter also addresses how formal, informal, and non-formal institutions are implicated in current efforts to redesign governing institutions in more culturally grounded and relevant ways. Finally, the chapter examines the relationship between civil society engagement and inclusive democratic governance. Indigenous movements have played a decisive role in determining the extent and nature of democratic inclusion in Bolivia, Ecuador, Nunavut, and Yukon. The inclusion of Indigenous actors in the structures of the state has produced deeper, more meaningful forms of democracy in each of the four cases.

## Indigenous Autonomy and Self-Government

Autonomy is the articulating claim of Indigenous peoples around the world. The demand for autonomy centres on the call for self-determination and self-government within Indigenous territories (Díaz Polanco 1998). Following González (2015, 17), Indigenous autonomy is understood in this study to refer to (a) the transfer of decision-making authority and administrative power to local collectives; (b) the establishment of self-governing political institutions within a recognized jurisdiction; and (c) the delimitation of territorial rights, including control over land and natural resources. According to Sambo Dorough (2021), the right to autonomy and self-government is central to the survival of Indigenous peoples as distinct peoples or nations. In Canada, Bolivia, and Ecuador, Indigenous autonomies have been recognized by the state and constituted as political-administrative units at the sub-national level (González et al. 2021). The demand for plurinationality, as expressed in Latin America, calls for the sharing of power and the recognition of Indigenous sovereignty within the framework of the state (Resina de la Fuente 2012). Plurinationality involves the re-founding of regime institutions, the reconceptualization of the nation-state, and the reconfiguration of the political map on the basis of Indigenous participation, legal pluralism, and Indigenous autonomies (Acosta 2009; De Sousa Santos 2009; Walsh 2009). Decolonization is perhaps best understood as a collective endeavour on the part of Indigenous peoples inspired by and oriented around the question of land (Singh 2019; Tuck and Wang 2012). Theoretically, decolonization is achieved when there is a nation-to-nation relationship between Indigenous peoples and the state on shared land. As Rivera Cusicanqui (2020, 49) asks, "How can the exclusive, ethnocentric 'we' be articulated with the inclusive 'we'—a homeland for everyone—that envisions decolonization?"

The work of Abele and Prince (2006) on pathways to Indigenous self-determination in Canada provides us with an important conceptual framework for comparing models of self-government. The authors identify four models or approaches to self-government that embody lesser to greater degrees of autonomy from the state: (a) mini-municipality; (b) public government as Indigenous self-government; (c) Indigenous governance as a third order of government; and (d) nation-to-nation relations or dual federations. The mini-municipality model envisions Indigenous governments as equivalent to local governments in size and governing authority. Under this model, Indigenous governments enjoy devolved administrative responsibilities while sovereignty continues to be shared between national and provincial or, in the case of northern Canada, territorial governments. According to Abele and Prince (2006, 586), the mini-municipality model has few supporters among Indigenous peoples. Likewise, the adapted federalism model, which proposes the creation of a new public government as opposed to an Indigenous-only government, is also based on a notion of sovereignty that is shared between national and provincial or territorial governments. However, this model does entail significant change to the national political map. In contrast, the third-order-of-government approach calls for the participation of Indigenous governments in the broader political system as a distinct order of government within the Canadian federation. In this scenario, sovereignty is shared between three orders of government. Lastly, the nation-to-nation approach to self-government is based on the concept of a parallel set of sovereign federations in a given territory. Instead of Indigenous nations and governments having power under or within the federal system, the dual federations model is based on the concept of power alongside the Canadian federation (Abele and Prince 2006, 584–5).

Abele and Prince's (2006) conceptual framework may fruitfully be applied to the case studies of this book. Table 1.1 depicts the different models of Indigenous autonomy and self-government in Bolivia, Ecuador, Nunavut, and Yukon. The case of the Yukon best approximates the nation-to-nation model.[1] The 1990 Umbrella Final Agreement provides the framework within which each of the fourteen Yukon First Nations may negotiate a First Nation Final Agreement (FNFA) that includes a range of common shared provisions as well as provisions unique to each First Nation (Alcantara 2013; Rice 2014a). FNFAs set out the tenure and management of settlement land as well as the rules regarding use of non-settlement land. On Category A Settlement Land (approximately 25,900 km$^2$), First Nations have ownership of the surface and subsurface, while on Category B Settlement Land (approximately 15,540 km$^2$) they have ownership and control only over the surface (CYFN and YTG 1997, 3). A Self-Government Agreement (SGA) accompanies each FNFA. The SGA outlines the powers, authorities, and responsibilities of the individual First Nation government. Under the SGA, a First Nation has the power to make and enact laws with respect to their lands and citizens (Coates and Morrison 2008). The various Indigenous and non-Indigenous governments work together through a territorial body called the Yukon Forum to avoid duplication of services and programs and to ensure that the needs of all citizens are being met. In matters of federal policy, an intergovernmental forum brings together federal ministers along with the Yukon premier and First Nation government leaders (Rice 2014a). The completion of the FNFAs and SGAs has clearly changed Indigenous-state relations in the territory.

In Bolivia, the practice of Indigenous autonomy and self-government best resembles the third-order-of-government model. The administration of Evo Morales (2006–19) committed itself to deepening the decentralization process that began in the mid-1990s as part of a package of neoliberal multicultural policies. The 1994 Law of Popular Participation created over three hundred municipal governments with widespread administrative powers,

**Table 1.1** Models of Indigenous autonomy and self-government

| Model | Example | Power Relations |
|---|---|---|
| Nation-to-nation | Yukon | Power alongside the state |
| Third order | Bolivia | Power within the state |
| Public government | Nunavut | Less power within the state |
| Mini-municipality | Ecuador | Power under the authority and control of the state |

*Source*: Abele and Prince (2006, 585).

direct citizen oversight, and dedicated resources as a means to bring government closer to increasingly mobilized rural and Indigenous communities (Arce and Rice 2009; Postero 2007). The reforms opened the door to the electoral participation of a new generation of Indigenous leaders, including Morales. As the governing party, the Movement toward Socialism under Morales instituted additional reforms that granted a substantial degree of autonomy to departmental, regional, municipal, and Indigenous governments (Centellas 2010; Faguet 2014). The 2010 Framework Law of Autonomy and Decentralization regulates the new territorial organization of the state as defined in the 2009 constitution. In addition to the recognition of the three hierarchical levels of government in Bolivia (i.e., departmental, regional, and municipal), the constitution also identified Indigenous autonomies as a separate and distinct order of government, one that is not directly subordinate to the other levels (CIPCA 2009). Under current provisions, existing Indigenous territories as well as municipalities and regions with a substantial Indigenous presence may convert themselves into self-governing entities based on cultural norms, customs, institutions, and authorities in keeping with the rights and guarantees in the new constitution (Faguet 2014, 6).

The case of Nunavut exemplifies Abele and Prince's (2006) model of public government as Indigenous self-government. The Nunavut Land Claims Agreement (NLCA) provided Inuit with title to more than 350,000 km$^2$ of land (equivalent to 18 per cent of Nunavut), subsurface mineral rights to approximately 36,000 km$^2$ of that land, and over CAD$1 billion in federal compensation money (DIAND 1997; Henderson 2009). Inuit beneficiaries of the claim are also entitled to a share of the royalties from oil and gas extraction on public lands, additional hunting and fishing rights, and the guaranteed right to participate in decisions over land and resource management. In exchange, Inuit had to surrender all existing and possibly existing surface and subsurface land rights in the area covered by the claim. The NLCA also committed the federal government to introduce a measure to create a new territory out of the existing Northwest Territories (Timpson 2009b; White 2006). The creation of the new territory brought with it the task of establishing a new territorial government. Given the disproportionate size and relative homogeneity of their population, as well as the greater likelihood of federal government support, Inuit decided on a system of public government (one that serves Indigenous and non-Indigenous peoples) instead of a more direct form of Inuit self-government (Rice 2016).

Finally, the practice of Indigenous autonomy and self-government in Ecuador most closely approximates the mini-municipality model. Although the 2008 constitution formally recognized the plurinational nature of the Ecuadorian state, its model of plurinational constitutionalism is quite limited in comparison to Bolivia's. For instance, Spanish remains Ecuador's official language (article 2), with Indigenous languages recognized only in the realm of intercultural relations (Schilling-Vacaflor and Kuppe 2012, 360). In addition, while both countries recognize Indigenous or customary law, the Bolivian constitution places ordinary and customary legal systems on an equal footing (article 179), whereas the Ecuadorian constitution does not (Wolff 2012, 192). Ecuador's new constitution recognizes Indigenous territories as jurisdictions that may take on the same responsibilities as those of local governments (Ortiz-T. 2021). It falls silent on the matter of guaranteed proportional representation for Indigenous peoples in the legislature and on the explicit recognition of the right to self-determination and self-government (Radcliffe 2012, 243). It also fails to open up participatory spaces for Indigenous actors within the structures of the state. Perhaps most telling, in Ecuador, as in Bolivia, the state retains control over the exploitation of non-renewable resources in Indigenous territories.

## Democratic Decolonization

In this study, the term "democratic decolonization" refers to the re-valorization, recognition, and re-establishment of Indigenous cultures, traditions, and values within the institutions, rules, and arrangements that govern society (Vice Ministerio de Descolonización 2013). According to Bolivia's vice minister of decolonization, Félix Cárdenas, the Bolivian state has not only historically excluded Indigenous peoples—it was in fact founded in opposition to them.[2] The same can, and should, be said of all settler states. The project of democratic decolonization entails reimagining the state and democracy. This means not only infusing the state with Indigenous principles and practices, but attempting to create new political subjects and forms of citizenship (Canessa 2012; García Linera 2014; Rice 2016). According to Ecuadorian Indigenous leader Luis Macas (2009, 97), "We cannot have a political project just for Indigenous peoples. To change the country we need to have a relationship with the broader society and a mechanism of exchange." In a similar vein, Canadian Indigenous scholar Glen Coulthard (2014, 179) suggests that "settler-colonialism has rendered us a radical minority in our own homelands and this necessitates that we continue to engage with the state's legal and political system." Finding an effective mechanism of Indigenous engagement with the state is crucial to decolonizing democracy. Borrowing from Roberts's (1998) conception of deepening democracy as an inherently continuous rather than discrete variable, decolonizing democracy revolves around the central analytical dimension of Indigenous autonomy that may contract or expand over time depending on the extent of Indigenous peoples' control over their own affairs.

Decolonization places new demands on democracy. Liberal or representative democracy—with its reliance on elections and parties as the only available channels of communication between representatives and citizens—does not require citizen deliberation on policy matters or collective action. According to Cameron (2014, 5), "Without a voice in deliberations over the decisions that may affect them directly, many citizens become disengaged. This malaise may be especially acute in [I]ndigenous communities with strong traditions of collective decision making." Institutional innovation is crucial to making democracy work for all sectors of society. Democratic innovations are institutional arrangements that open up the policy-making process to citizen participation, deliberation, and decision making (Smith 2009; Talpin 2015). Comprehensive land claims with self-government agreements in the North and the introduction of elements of communitarian democracy and Indigenous governance principles in the constitutions of the South are key democratic innovations that have provided important measures of self-determination for Indigenous peoples. Self-determination challenges an institutional context that shapes and constrains Indigenous participation (Eversole 2010). As Montúfar (2006) points out, agents of representative democracy are reluctant to innovate given their commitment to the principle of political

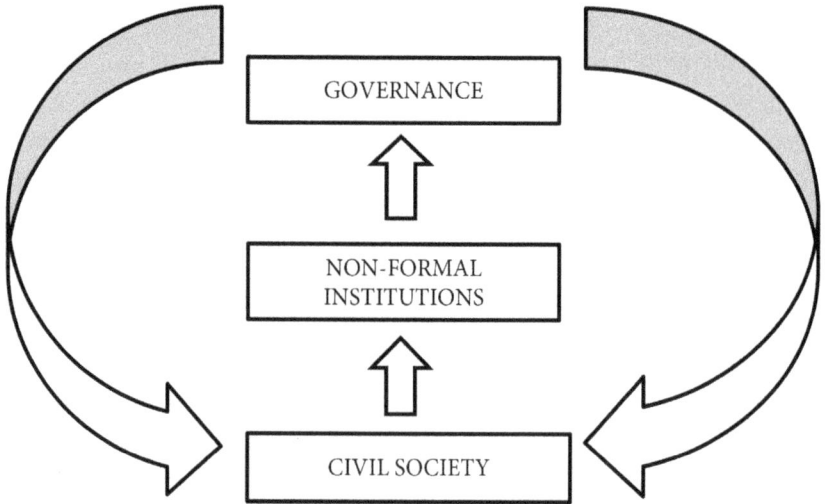

**Figure 1.1** Process of democratic decolonization

responsibility and the performance-based evaluation criteria that guide their actions. Unlike political parties, civil society organizations have greater liberty to propose and act on new initiatives as their legitimacy is derived from internal consensus rather than external approval. Decolonizing democracy thus requires that civil society actors drive change and that institutions are grounded in, or at least made compatible with, the traditions and values of the peoples they serve (Eversole 2010).

Figure 1.1 illustrates, in ideal terms, the process for decolonizing democracy. Based on the findings from the comparative case studies presented in this book, the critical components of a decolonized democratic system include the following: (1) an actively engaged civil society that pressures for institutional change; (2) non-formal institutions as the site of political innovation; and (3) the dispersal of governing authority beyond the traditional centres of power. Decolonizing democracy means that representation and participation may occur beyond, and at times outside, the traditional channels of representation. Nevertheless, while the shift to a decolonized democratic system may change the character of representative democracy, it need not be seen as undermining it (Cameron, Hershberg, and Sharpe 2012; Exeni

Rodríguez 2012). New mechanisms for Indigenous inclusion and representation have the potential to strengthen representative democracy by enhancing or stretching liberal democratic conceptions and expectations (Anria 2016; Della Porta 2013).

## Governance and the State

Democratic decolonization is closely intertwined with the concept of governance. Governance can be understood as "the structures and processes that enable governmental and nongovernmental actors to coordinate their interdependent needs and interests through the making and implementation of policies in the absence of a unifying political authority" (Krahmann 2003, 331). In other words, whereas government centralizes power in the state, governance disperses political authority among governmental and non-governmental actors, as well as Indigenous communities, in potentially democratizing ways (Swyngedouw 2005). It is the process through which governments, civil society organizations, and private-sector associations interact and make decisions on matters of public concern (Graham, Amos, and Plumptre 2003; Levi-Faur 2012). To promote the growth of society-centred governance, governments must be willing to work in partnership with civil society at each stage of the policy design and implementation process. The practise of public dialogue and deliberation is both a means and an opportunity to bridge the gap that exists between formal democratic institutions and excluded Indigenous communities and their public authorities (Retolaza Eguren 2008).

Decolonizing democracy requires the restoration of Indigenous forms of governance, ethics, and philosophies that arise from relationships on and with the land, including the natural world (Alfred 2009; Singh 2019). As Acosta (2009) has pointed out, democratic decolonization is not only an exercise in democratic inclusion; it is above all a proposal for a diverse way of life that is in greater harmony with nature. In this way, the debate over how to decolonize democracy must include discussions about land and natural resource governance. If settler colonialism is fundamentally about dispossessing Indigenous peoples from the land, then the project of decolonization must include actions and practices that reconnect Indigenous peoples to the land (Wildcat et al. 2014). One means of re-establishing Indigenous control over territory and governance is state recognition of and respect for the principle of free, prior, and informed consent (FPIC). The right to FPIC—or "prior consultation," as it is known in Latin America—is established in international conventions, notably the International Labour Organization's Convention 169 on Indigenous and Tribal Peoples (1989) and in non-binding or soft law, such as the 2007 United Nations Declaration on the Rights of Indigenous Peoples. FPIC is a global standard against which governments can be measured in their interactions with Indigenous peoples concerning planned measures affecting their communities, such as mineral, oil, and gas exploitation (Resina de la Fuente 2012; Szablowski 2010). A prior consent regime, as opposed to a consultation regime, involves the sharing or transfer of authority between extractive industry project proponents and Indigenous communities in nation-to-nation-type negotiations (Rice 2019). The power to support or reject a project serves to enhance a community's negotiating power, strengthen its internal governance processes, and ensures a more equitable outcome.

New institutional arrangements to promote the participation of Indigenous peoples in the political decision-making process in northern Canada and the central Andes, such as natural resource co-management boards and Indigenous-centred public policies, are challenging conventional state-centric forms of policy-making and generating new forms of society-centred governance (Clarke 2017; Smith 2009). The Governments of Bolivia, Nunavut, Yukon, and to a lesser extent Ecuador, aim to decolonize democracy by incorporating Indigenous voices and values into their respective political systems. In so doing, they offer important instructional lessons in how to institutionalize Indigenous rights, world views, and governing principles within liberal democratic orders. The case studies demonstrate that a significant political institutional space or opening is needed for bold experiments in Indigenous governance to occur. For instance, in the cases of Bolivia and Nunavut, Indigenous peoples were presented with the opportunity to build a new government, practically from the ground up. This particular confluence of factors has allowed democratic and Indigenous governance innovations to flourish.

## Formal and Non-formal Institutions

In Canada and Latin America, formal or state institutions of representative democracy (e.g., political parties, elections, legislatures, courts) coexist and compete with vibrant yet marginalized traditional and adapted Indigenous governance structures and institutions (e.g., customary law and communal justice; leaders and authorities; land-use and -tenure practices). According to Retolaza Eguren (2008, 313), "at one extreme, we have Western-minded formal institutions with strong public funding as well as funding from international donors and lenders; at the other extreme, self-sustained or underfunded non-formal institutions which sternly condition [I]ndigenous and peasant social and political life and hence its interaction with the wider context." In much of Latin America, the uneven reach of the state and formal democracy has excluded Indigenous and rural people while providing them with a de facto form of autonomy (Lucero 2012). A similar dynamic is witnessed in northern Canada, where Indigenous groups are remote from the seat of power and have experienced a much less intensive and protracted process of citizenship than their southern counterparts (Henderson 2008; Milen 1991). The governance gap that exists between these historically excluded Indigenous communities and formal public authorities and institutions has undermined the legitimacy and performance of democratic institutions.

Institutions comprise the underlying "rules of the game" that organize social, political, and economic relations within a polity (North 1990). Indigenous governance institutions are distinct from formal and informal institutions. *Formal institutions* are the written rules and regulations, such as constitutions, laws, and policies, that are enforced by officially recognized authorities. Much of the literature on democracy and development focuses on how formal institutions shape political actions and outcomes (e.g., Mainwaring and Scully 1995; March and Olsen 1989; Rothstein 1996). This body of literature fails to note the important influence that informal and non-formal institutions have on actor expectations and behaviours in practice. *Informal institutions* are socially shared rules and regulations, usually unwritten, that are created, communicated, and enforced outside officially sanctioned channels (Levitsky 2012; O'Donnell 1996). *Non-formal* or *non-state institutions* are neither informally constituted nor formally recognized by the state. They include customary laws and practices and traditional authority and governance structures (Eversole 2010; Retolaza Eguren 2008). Whereas the emerging literature on informal institutions is divided over whether or not informal practices, such as clientelism and patrimonialism, compete with or complement the performance of formal institutions, the role of non-formal institutions in making formal democratic institutions work has yet to be addressed (Levitsky 2012).

The cultural foundations of institutions of Indigenous governance, however, are not without controversy. Recent scholarship on multiculturalism and Indigenous rights has focused on the perceived tension between collective and individual rights. On the one hand, the recognition of the collective Indigenous right to autonomy is suggested to serve as an important corrective to the assimilationist and integrationist policies and practices of the past. On the other hand, it is argued that local autonomous spaces may come at the expense of community members' constitutionally protected individual rights, especially women's rights (Danielson and Eisenstadt 2009). According to Lucero (2013, 33), "while one should avoid any romantic notions about Indigenous spaces, it is also important to avoid the opposite mistake of seeing them as the static containers of 'tradition' and take a closer look to see how Indigenous men and women continue to transform what it means to be 'Indigenous,' 'men,' and 'women.'" Broadly speaking, Indigenous people cannot enjoy their individual rights without first securing their collective rights (Regino Montes and Torres Cisneros 2009). Coates and Morrison (2008) have suggested that even though self-government rooted in traditional philosophies and practices may not be democratic in the liberal sense, it seems to serve the needs of the communities by helping to educate Indigenous youth in the traditional ways, broadening community debates, and providing for greater potential inclusion in governance processes. Official acknowledgement of the important role played by non-state institutions within Indigenous communities is essential to promoting Indigenous engagement with the broader formal political environment.

## Citizenship and Agency

Democratic and Indigenous governance innovation demands an active citizenry. Political will and inclusive democratic institutions, while necessary, are in themselves insufficient to decolonize democracy. Citizens must take on the role of protagonists by demanding and defending their rights, seeking greater social control of their governments, working with the institutions of democracy, and by leading political innovation (Beatriz Ruiz 2007; Montúfar 2007). In the words of Guillermo O'Donnell (2010, 197), "this construction entails, and legally demands, the effectuation of a system of respectful mutual recognition as such citizens/agents in our legitimate diversity." Agency and citizenship are at the core of democracy. Given that citizens bring with them dense networks of social relations, collective affiliations, cultures, and identities, there cannot be a single, superior model of democracy; indeed, there are many variations and pathways to further democratization (O'Donnell 2010). Democratic innovations, such as self-government, popular assemblies, or participatory budget councils, open an important space so that citizen initiatives can influence formal institutions and processes, which in turn allows for the development of a more active citizenry (Lupien 2016; Oxhorn 2016). Mechanisms of Indigenous collaboration with formal authorities on key policy matters do not imply the erosion of representation or the substitution of the roles and responsibilities of political parties, but rather the development of a synergistic relationship between Indigenous communities and the state.

Struggles over citizenship have profound consequences for state-society relations. Oxhorn (2011) has identified three broad models of citizenship: citizenship as co-optation; citizenship as consumption; and citizenship as agency. *Citizenship as co-optation* refers to the historical tendency of Latin American elites to grant citizenship rights selectively so as to control and contain popular-sector demands for socio-economic equality and political inclusion. For Indigenous people, this meant national incorporation into the political system as peasants in the 1960s and '70s as a means to access land, credit, and services from the state under a corporatist citizenship regime (Yashar 2005). The shift to neoliberal economic policies in the 1980s and '90s resulted in the weakening of state corporatist institutions and the move to more atomized or individuated state-society relations as part of a neoliberal citizenship regime. *Citizenship as consumption* understands citizens as consumers who spend their votes and resources to access minimal rights of democratic citizenship in a market-oriented environment (Oxhorn 2011, 32). Both citizenship as co-optation and citizenship as consumption heavily circumscribe the role of civil society in democratic governance. In contrast, *citizenship as agency* involves the active participation of civil society actors in public policy deliberation, design, and implementation. Active citizenship entails a process of democratic learning, for civil society actors as well as for political authorities, that has the potential to generate new understandings of social reality and ways of doing democracy (Montúfar 2007). According to Oxhorn (2011, 30), "citizenship as agency ideally reflects the active role that multiple actors, particularly those representing disadvantaged groups, must play in the social construction of citizenship so that democratic governance can realize its full potential." Only citizenship as agency has the capacity bring about democratic decolonization.

Collective action has been the principal historical motor for the expansion and universalization of civil, political, and economic rights. In Latin

America, Indigenous movements have organized national strikes and protests, blocked neoliberal reforms, and in some instances formed political parties and even captured presidencies (Albó 2002; Bengoa 2000; Lucero 2008; Van Cott 2005; Yashar 2005). In Canada, Indigenous peoples have participated in constitutional reforms, negotiated land claims, won policy concessions, and secured an important measure of self-determination (Abele and Prince 2003; Cairns 2000; Cameron and White 1995; Henderson 2007; Ladner and Orsini 2003). As the cases under consideration in this study indicate, Indigenous autonomy and institutional participation do not have to be mutually exclusive. Civil society can play a critical role in facilitating innovations in democratic governance by working with the state on policy matters, setting new public agendas, and advocating for institutional change in the corridors of power.

## Conclusion

This chapter aimed to outline the book's main theoretical and conceptual stance on how to decolonize democracy. It also provided a glimpse into the different models and approaches to Indigenous autonomy and self-government in Canada and Latin America that will be examined in the chapters that follow. Strong and cohesive Indigenous movements pressing for institutional change are suggested to be the motor of political innovation in Bolivia, Ecuador, Nunavut, and Yukon. Mutual respect and recognition between the state and Indigenous actors appear to be critical ingredients for strengthening Indigenous autonomy and self-government. The chapter proposed that Indigenous governance innovation plays an important role in improving the quality of formal institutions, which in turn can aid democratic governability and advance Indigenous rights agendas. Decolonizing democracy requires new institutions that provide the space for an active partnership between Indigenous actors and the state in the pursuit of common goals (Oxhorn 2011). In Bolivia, Ecuador, Nunavut, and Yukon, an unparalleled space and political push for democratic innovation has resulted in efforts to incorporate Indigenous or non-formal institutions into formal democratic arrangements. This has broadened the inclusive qualities of their respective democracies. The shallow reach of representative democracy in Indigenous communities in Canada and Latin America has created a fluid democratic landscape that is ripe for experimentation (Roberts 2016).

The case study chapters that follow reveal several challenges to the implementation of Indigenous autonomy and self-government in practice. First, while the cases highlight the gains that Indigenous peoples have derived from working within the system to push for positive change, as opposed to relying solely on extra-systemic tactics, they also demonstrate the need for political will by governing elites to address Indigenous rights demands—something that is in short supply throughout much of the Americas. Second, the case study chapters reveal the importance of establishing a secure land base, ideally with subsurface mineral rights, for self-determination and autonomy to be fully realized in practice. Finally, the cases demonstrate that there are serious tensions between Indigenous territorial autonomy and the resource-dependent, extractivist models of development pursued by the Governments of Canada, Bolivia, and Ecuador. Reconciling natural resource development with Indigenous sovereignty is a critical challenge for the Americas. Repairing and rebuilding Indigenous-state relations on a more just and equal footing requires recognition of and respect for the Indigenous right to autonomy and self-government. Indigenous governance arrangements of the variety explored here hold great potential to foster inclusive democratic processes in Canada, Latin America, and beyond. As the following chapters will demonstrate, there is much to celebrate in the four cases, just as there is much work left to do to make these visions of a more just society a reality.

# 2

# Yukon: Leading the World in Nation-to-Nation Indigenous Self-Government

*We want to cut the apron strings and get on with our lives.*
—Grand Chief Ruth Massie, Council of Yukon First Nations[1]

It is a common refrain among non-Indigenous Yukoners that the territory's First Nations "got away with murder" in negotiating their extensive powers of autonomy and self-government through the 1990 Umbrella Final Agreement (UFA), and that such a deal will never be seen again. How did Yukon First Nations achieve such a substantial degree of nation-to-nation self-governing powers? What lessons does this case teach us in terms of advancing Indigenous rights to autonomy and self-government? Addressing these questions is the central task of this chapter. The chapter refutes the notion that the achievements of Yukon First Nations are an anomaly, based on conditions of geography or circumstance that cannot be replicated. Instead, I suggest that strategic and effective interest representation on the part of Yukon First Nations played a key role in advancing Indigenous claims. According to Grand Chief Massie, quoted above in the epigraph, settling land claims in the North was not a matter of attaining a "free lunch," but rather the accomplishment of decades of struggle and negotiation with the Canadian government.

The aim of this chapter is to provide instructional lessons on how institutions, in theory and in practice, can be designed or constructed to achieve a nation-to-nation relationship between Indigenous peoples and the state. The Yukon case offers us an important example of a model of self-government that embodies relations of power alongside the state, as opposed to power within the state (Abele and Prince 2006, 585). In contemporary Yukon, First Nation governments have taken their place alongside the federal and territorial governments (Cameron and White 1995). Critics of the new institutional arrangement abound. While for some observers the deal "goes too far," for others it does not go far enough in terms of guaranteeing the fundamental rights of Indigenous peoples (Charlie 2020). The Yukon is a predominantly non-Indigenous territory. Even among the First Nations, which make up almost one-quarter of the total population of the territory, there are significant differences between linguistic and cultural groupings and in social and political priorities (Rice 2014a). Three of the Yukon's fourteen First Nations—White River First Nation, Liard First Nation, Ross River Dena Council—have yet to conclude land claims and self-government agreements. The Kaska people of Liard First Nation and Ross River Dena Council, for example, take issue with the cede, release, and surrender clause with regard to their traditional territory that is outlined in the UFA, suggesting that the agreement does not offer enough land to meet their cultural needs (Alcantara 2013). In the words of one First Nation government staffer, "The Yukon is a big social experiment; one that has completely changed the relationship between Aboriginal and non-Aboriginal people."[2]

The chapter begins with a brief political history of the Yukon, with a particular emphasis on the role of resource extraction in stimulating Indigenous political organization and mobilization in defence of Indigenous lands. The chapter then turns to the comprehensive land claims process in the territory to advance our understanding of how this historic agreement was reached before analyzing its far-reaching implications for Indigenous-state relations. The politics of self-government in the Yukon is then examined. Self-governing First Nations are involved in a dual political project of building up capacity within their own communities while engaging in territorial party politics to ensure a political climate favourable to their interests. The chapter concludes with a discussion on lessons learned from Yukon First Nations in terms of advancing Indigenous rights to autonomy and self-government in an established democracy.

## Resource Extraction and Political Development

Yukon First Nations have had to struggle for control over their lands and livelihoods ever since the Klondike Gold Rush of the 1890s and the expansion of infrastructure, notably the construction of the Alaska Highway, during the Second World War brought a massive influx of outsiders to the territory (Coates and Morrison 2017). Bordering the state of Alaska to the west, the province of British Columbia to the south, the Northwest Territories to the east, and the Beaufort Sea of the Arctic Ocean to the north, the Yukon is Canada's smallest and westernmost territory. According to the latest census statistics, Yukon is home to 43,118 residents, with more than 78 per cent of them living in the capital city of Whitehorse and its surrounding area.[3] Although some of the Yukon First Nation communities number only in the hundreds in terms of population size, they are modern-day leaders of Indigenous self-government. More than half of Canada's self-governing First Nations are found in the Yukon (Alcantara 2007). The territory's political development has tended to follow on the heels of its economic development. The Yukon, along with the Northwest Territories and Nunavut, comprise nearly 40 per cent of Canada's land mass and contain vast amounts of renewable and non-renewable resources (Cameron and White 1995). The Yukon became a territory of Canada in 1898 with the passage of the Yukon Act. In 1902, Chief Jim Boss (Kishxóot) of the Ta'an Kwäch'än First Nation wrote a letter to the superintendent general of Indian affairs in Ottawa, Canada's capital, in which he stated, "Tell the King very hard, we want something for our Indians because they take our land and our game" (CYFN 2005, 1). The response from Ottawa was a promise that the police would protect his people and their land from intruders. This exchange of letters is regarded as the first attempt at land claim negotiations in the Yukon.[4]

The Indigenous peoples of the Yukon have traditionally relied upon the use of renewable resources in the form of hunting, trapping, and gathering on the land. The extraction of non-renewable resources, such as minerals, oil, and gas, tends to alienate Indigenous people from the land (Cameron and White 1995, 12). Indigenous ownership of and control over subsurface resource rights is especially pertinent in the Canadian case given the country's unusual free-entry claim (or "staking") process. Free-entry tenure under the Quartz Mining Act (2003) gives resource companies the right of entry and access to lands which have mineral potential on a first-come, first-served basis by simply staking a claim (now done electronically through the Mining Recorder's Office). According to Deneault and Sacher (2012), free-entry staking is rooted in colonial policy as a means to settle land. The free-entry approach was developed into law by England in the eighteenth century and brought by settlers to manage the gold rushes in California and the Yukon. Today, it serves as a means to circumvent the Indigenous consultation process (Cameron 2013). Only the Canadian provinces of Alberta and Prince Edward Island have eliminated free-entry staking. In Ontario, the free-entry principle has been modified such that mining companies are legally required to consult with Indigenous peoples prior to initiating exploration activities (Hart and Hoogeveen 2012). As a general rule, however, very few spaces in Canada are off-limits to free-entry staking, including the territories.

Jurisdiction over land and resources is a contentious issue in the North. Unlike the provinces, which enjoy their own autonomous powers and jurisdictions, the territories fall under the legislative authority of the federal government (Cameron and White 1995). Historically, this has meant that the North was largely governed by federal officials. Since the 1980s, however, major changes have occurred in the governance of the territories. Through the devolution of powers and responsibilities from the federal to the territorial governments, the territories are now accorded many of the privileges associated with provincial status (Alcantara 2013). For instance, each territory has its own premier and legislative assembly, which has the power to enact laws within its territory, and its own public service and court system. Territorial governments also now have jurisdiction over social services, such as health and education, and renewable resources, including forestry and wildlife. In contrast to the provinces, where Crown or public lands are provincially owned, the federal government owns public lands in the territories. As White (2020) has pointed out, this is of critical importance to territorial governance given that, aside from the lands owned by Indigenous peoples through their comprehensive land claims, the territories consist almost entirely of Crown land. On April 1, 2003, the Yukon made history when it became the first Canadian territory to take over land- and resource-management responsibilities through the completion of the Yukon Devolution Transfer Agreement. With the exception of Indigenous settlement lands with subsurface rights, the one major power that the federal government has retained over the territories is ownership of non-renewable resources (White 2020, 22).

The contemporary Indigenous movement in the Yukon can be traced back to the 1973 ruling by the Supreme Court of Canada, known as the Calder decision, that recognized the existence of Indigenous title to land prior to colonization (Belanger 2008; Sabin 2014). In that year, Chief Elijah Smith of Kwanlin Dün First Nation renewed the call for increased control on the part of First Nations over their territories and governing affairs following the publication of the visionary document entitled *Together Today for Our Children Tomorrow: A Statement of Grievances and an Approach to Settlement* (CYI 1973). Chief Smith, along with a delegation of other Yukon chiefs, travelled to Ottawa to present the document to then prime minister Pierre Trudeau and his minister of Indian affairs. In his speech to the prime minister, Chief Smith stated the following:

> This is the first time the leaders of the Yukon Indian people have come to the capital of Canada. We are here to talk about the future. The only way we feel we can have a future, is to settle our land claim. This be a future that will return to us our lost pride, self-respect, and economic independence. We are not here for a handout. We are here with a plan. (CYFN 2005, ii)

The position of the chiefs represented a significant breakthrough in terms of the conceptualization of self-government in Canada. They asserted the importance of establishing a land base, and thus economic self-sufficiency, before becoming self-governing. According to Belanger and Newhouse (2008, 6), this was the first time in Canada that the link between land and self-government was explicitly made. Together, the chiefs were able to convince the federal government to negotiate a land claim agreement with the Yukon First Nations.

## Levelling the Playing Field: Comprehensive Land Claims

The Council for Yukon Indians (CYI) was born out of the collective struggle for Indigenous autonomy and self-government. In 1975, the CYI was formally incorporated as a non-governmental organization with an official mandate to negotiate and complete a Yukon land claim on behalf of the fourteen First Nations with the Government of Canada (Jensen 2005). The central goal of the CYI was to secure a land base for Yukon First Nations as a foundation for self-government. It sought to achieve this by aggregating the interests of the First Nations at a regional level in a context in which First Nations have historically maintained distinct identities, as well as a desire for various forms of self-government that reflect this diversity (Cameron and White 1995). To be effective, the CYI had to engage in a mode of interest mediation akin to diplomatic relations between the various First Nations and the federal and later territorial governments. The outcome of land claim negotiations may be subject to multiple factors, including the relative bargaining strength of the parties involved, the quality of leadership, a favourable political and legal context, and the commercial value of the land in question and its proximity to urban centres (Morse 2008). As Alcantara (2007) has noted, the comprehensive land claims process places Indigenous peoples in a weaker position relative to that of settler governments by forcing them to adopt Western forms of knowledge, discourse, and standards of proof to satisfy formal rules and procedures. A positive outcome depends on the ability of weaker actors (First Nations) to influence the stronger actors (federal and provincial/territorial governments). In the case of the Yukon land claim negotiations, the CYI managed to tip the scales in favour of the First Nations by effectively brokering their interests.

Throughout the 1980s, at the height of the CYI's political authority, the organization counted on more than a hundred employees and an annual budget of approximately $350,000 in core funding from the federal government to support its operations (CYFN 2005, 10). An elected chair and vice-chairs headed the CYI. Each was elected for two-year terms through a territory-wide First Nation vote. A General Assembly composed of First Nation representatives provided the CYI with direction. Land claim negotiations were conducted initially as a two-way exchange between the federal minister of Indian affairs and northern development and the CYI. In 1979, the Yukon Territorial Government became a party to the negotiations when it achieved status as a representative and responsible government and evolved into a "proto-province" with a significant degree of political autonomy (Cameron and White 1995). For its part, the CYI counted on the participation of strong, capable First Nation leaders, such as Dave Joe, in the negotiation process. Joe, the first Indigenous lawyer admitted to the Yukon bar, served as the CYI's chief negotiator from 1977 to 1984 (CYFN 2005). According to Lawrence Joe, executive director for the Champagne and Aishihik First Nations, a relative of Dave Joe, his people have always placed a strong emphasis on education and have invested in "gap students" who have not received enough formal schooling to obtain a government post.[5] The CYI's influence during this period extended to the national level, where it played a key role in the development of provisions in Canada's Constitution Act, 1982, pertaining to Indigenous self-government.

In January 1984, a tentative agreement was reached between the federal government, the territorial government, and the CYI. The agreement provided Yukon First Nations with a settlement of approximately $620 million to be paid over twenty years and 20,000 km$^2$ of land.[6] However, the agreement contained an extinguishment clause under which First Nations would be required to relinquish existing and possibly existing land rights to their remaining territories. The agreement also proposed a limited form of self-government in which First Nations would sit on boards and committees in an advisory capacity vis-à-vis the Yukon government, but the territorial government would have final say on all matters.[7] The minimal self-governing powers afforded by the agreement contravened the notion of self-government held by First Nations as well as that put forward by the Parliamentary Task Force on Indian Self-Government chaired by Member of Parliament Keith Penner the year prior. The resulting Penner report recommended the recognition of First Nations as a distinct, constitutionally recognized order of government within Canada with a wide range of powers (Belanger and Newhouse 2008). The tentative agreement went before the General Assembly of the CYI in August 1984, where it was rejected by its membership. When the CYI remained firm in its decision not to accept the agreement in the face of continued pressure from the federal government, talks between the two sides broke off. According to former chief of the Teslin Tlingit Council Sam Johnston, a key lesson of the negotiation process was to "read the small print too. And if it's not quite what you want, you wouldn't sign it."[8]

The rejection of the 1984 tentative agreement by the Council for Yukon Indians was a critical moment in the struggle for self-government. It represented the depth of the CYI's commitment to the type of self-government envisioned by First Nation communities and the unwillingness to waver on the part of Yukon First Nations. The CYI recognized the importance of working with institutional allies and taking advantage of favourable political junctures. When the Yukon section of the New Democratic Party (NDP), Canada's left-of-centre social democratic organization, formed a minority government in 1985 under the leadership of Tony Penikett, an advocate of Indigenous and workers' rights, the CYI seized the opportunity to re-initiate negotiations.[9] In 1988, the Yukon government, the CYI, and the federal government reached a new agreement-in-principle. It provided for $242 million to be paid to First Nations over fifteen years, approximately 25,900 km$^2$ of land, and the development of a transformational model of self-government. Although the new agreement provided far less compensation money, the promise of self-government and the additional land base led to its ratification by First Nation communities.[10] After the 1989 territorial elections, the NDP formed a majority government with Penikett as premier, the first Yukon government leader to assume this title.

In 1990, the Umbrella Final Agreement was finalized. It was formally signed by the three parties in 1993. The UFA provided the framework within which each of the fourteen Yukon First Nations could negotiate a First Nation Final Agreement (FNFA) that would include a range of common shared provisions as well as specific provisions unique to each First Nation. The FNFAs are highly significant as they are constitutionally protected legal agreements between the Government of Canada, the Government of Yukon, and individual First Nations that may only be amended with the consent of all three parties (CYFN and YTG 1997). The signing of the individual FNFA marked the conclusion of the treaty-negotiation process for that First Nation. By 1993, four First Nations had reached their final agreements: the First Nation of Na-Cho Nyäk Dun in Mayo, Champagne and Aishihik First Nations in Haines Junction, the Vuntut Gwitchin First Nation in Old Crow, and the Teslin Tlingit Council in Teslin. By 1998, the Little Salmon-Carmacks First Nation in Carmacks, Selkirk First Nation in Pelly Crossing, and Tr'ondëk Hwëch'in First Nation in Dawson City had signed their own agreements and become self-governing First Nations. In 2002, the Ta'an Kwäch'än Council in Whitehorse signed its agreement. In 2003, the Kluane First Nation in Burwash Landing reached its final agreement. By 2005, the Kwanlin Dün First Nation in Whitehorse and the Carcross/Tagish First Nation in Carcross had finalized their agreements. The three remaining First Nations (White River First Nation, Liard First Nation, and Ross River Dena Council) have yet to complete their FNFAs.

Yukon FNFAs set out the tenure and management of settlement land as well as the rules regarding use of non-settlement land. On Category A settlement land, First Nations have ownership of the surface and subsurface. On Category B settlement land, First Nations have only the right to use the surface of the land. While First Nations do not have ownership of subsurface minerals, oil, and gas on Category B land, they do have the right to take and use certain specified substances without payment of royalties (CYFN and YTG 1997, 3). The combined total of Category A settlement lands allocated to First Nation communities is 25,000 km², equivalent to 5.4 per cent of Yukon's total land

**Table 2.1** Allocation of Yukon First Nation settlement land by square kilometre under the Umbrella Final Agreement (1990)

| First Nation | Category A* | Category B** |
|---|---|---|
| Carcross/Tagish | 1,036.00 | 518.00 |
| Champagne and Aishihik | 1,230.24 | 1,165.49 |
| Kluane | 647.50 | 259.00 |
| Kwanlin Dün | 647.50 | 388.50 |
| Liard | 2,408.69 | 2,330.99 |
| Little Salmon/Carmacks | 1,553.99 | 1,036.00 |
| Na-Cho Nyäk Dun | 2,408.69 | 2,330.99 |
| Ross River Dena | 2,382.79 | 2,330.99 |
| Selkirk | 2,408.69 | 2,330.99 |
| Ta'an Kwäch'än | 388.50 | 388.50 |
| Teslin Tlingit | 1,230.24 | 1,165.49 |
| Tr'ondëk Hwëch'in | 1,553.99 | 1,036.00 |
| Vuntut Gwitchin | 7,744.06 | 0 |
| White River | 259.00 | 259.00 |
| **TOTAL** | **25,899.88** | **15,539.93** |

*Category A: First Nations have ownership of the surface and subsurface
**Category B: First Nations have ownership of the surface only
*Source*: Fred (n.d., 4).

area (see table 2.1).[11] Category B settlement lands consist of 15,540 km$^2$ or 3.2 per cent of the territory's total land area. The Vuntut Gwitchin First Nation, the Yukon's northernmost rural community, received the largest Category A land settlement in the negotiation process (7,744 km$^2$). It was also one of the first to reach its final agreement. The urban-based First Nations located in the capital city of Whitehorse, Ta'an Kwäch'än and Kwanlin Dün, received comparatively small land allocations (389 km$^2$ and 648 km$^2$, respectively) given their proximity to the urban core, and they were some of the last First Nations to finalize their agreements. Although Indigenous title is ceded, released, and surrendered (as opposed to extinguished) on non-settlement land, Yukon First Nations retain considerable subsistence rights to public lands as well as the right of access to their traditional routes (CYFN and YTG 1997, 14). In terms of the Yukon's free-entry staking system, the holder of an existing mineral claim on Category A settlement land that predates the signing of an FNFA has a right of access to exercise mineral rights without the consent of the First Nation provided that the intervention does not result in significant alteration to the land. New mineral interests on Category A settlement lands, including staking, exploration, and exploitation, are governed by the First Nations.[12]

The UFA also laid out a revenue-sharing arrangement with First Nations for extractive sector operations on their lands. Yukon First Nations receive all of the royalties from any resource development on Category A settlement land. For Category B settlement land, however, the revenue-sharing formula is different. In this case, the resource royalties from subsurface mineral operations go to the Yukon government. The territorial government is required to share the royalties it receives with all First Nations, but only by the amount that exceeds the total amount of royalties received by First Nations from their Category A settlement land (Forrest 2016). This revenue-sharing arrangement has generated considerable discontent among First Nations, who lose out when one First Nation manages to generate more resource royalties than the Yukon government. For instance, the Minto Mine copper-gold mine located on Selkirk First Nation Category A settlement land, which went into operation in 2007, is estimated to have generated close to $5.9 million in resource royalties for the First Nation by 2010 (Prno 2013). Given that the Selkirk First Nation has been earning more in resource royalties than the Yukon government for a number of years, the government has not been sharing its royalties with any First Nation in the territory. This regressive revenue-sharing formula may create institutional incentives for First Nations to consent to new mining projects within their settlement lands. As analysts have noted, there is a correlation between the settlement of comprehensive land claims and an increase in extractive activities in Canada given the exchange of undefined Indigenous rights for formally defined rights and benefits (Aragón 2015; Rodon 2017).

One of the most significant governance innovations to date in terms of restructuring Indigenous-state relations in the Yukon has been the territory's co-management and regulatory system. The co-management boards on land-use planning, wildlife management, and environmental regulation were mandated by the UFA (see table 2.2). The boards are institutions of public government, as opposed to a form of Indigenous self-government, that ensure Indigenous participation in key policy decisions while maintaining government control over the use and management of public lands (Cameron and White 1995). According to White (2020, 4), co-management boards represent

**Table 2.2** Yukon land claim boards

| Board name | Seats |
| --- | --- |
| Environment and Socio-economic Assessment Board | 7 |
| Fish and Wildlife Management Board | 12 |
| Land Use Planning Council | 3 |
| Salmon Sub-committee | 10 |
| Surface Rights Board | 5 |
| Water Board | 9 |

*Source:* White (2020, 41).

a compromise between Indigenous peoples' demands for control over matters of crucial importance to their lives and the exercise of state power. The jurisdiction of the boards extends to the entirety of the Yukon (not just to First Nation settlement lands), though their powers are limited to making recommendations to the government minister responsible for that portfolio (Nadasdy 2003). While the boards may only have advisory powers, their decisions are rarely overturned by the government. The participatory resource governance provisions contained within the UFA speak not only to the importance of land and resources for Yukon First Nations, but also to the desire to integrate their interests with those of the general public. Cameron and White (1995, 29) suggest that the completion of the comprehensive land claim has " 'levelled the playing field' for the Yukon's Aboriginal people in that neither governments nor private resource developers can henceforth ignore their confirmed role in the management of the territory's land and resources."

## The Politics of Self-Governing First Nations

A Self-Government Agreement (SGA) accompanies each of the First Nation Final Agreements. The SGAs are not constitutionally protected documents. The SGA outlines the powers, authorities, and responsibilities of the individual First Nation governments in such areas as taxation, municipal planning, and the management and co-management of land and resources. It also provides for funding in support of program and service delivery at the First Nation level. As Coates and Morrison (2008) point out, the agreements are flexible in the sense that Indigenous authorities are not required to assume any or all of the governing powers available to them, nor are there timelines imposed on the transfer of federal or territorial responsibilities to First

Nation governments. The agreements are also multidirectional, meaning that self-governing First Nations can accept those powers when they deem them appropriate but can also return them to the territorial or federal government if needed. Under the SGA, a First Nation has the power to make and enact laws with respect to their lands and citizens.[13] First Nation law-making powers are not subject to those of the other governments. Describing the negotiation of the UFA, the legal counsel for the Government of Yukon offered the following reflection on the new legal regime:

> When we were negotiating that [the displacement model] we actually thought . . . we, being [the] Yukon Government, is this what we want? Are we willing to take that risk that the First Nations will have laws that we don't like and don't want . . . ? And we just came to the conclusion that . . . that's what happens when you deal with another government. You're not always going to agree. And governments have the right to make laws in respect of their people and in respect of their land that make sense for them, even if it's not what we might want.[14]

The various governments work together through a local body called the Yukon Forum to avoid duplication of services and programs and to ensure that the needs of all of the territory's citizens are met.[15] In matters of federal policy, an intergovernmental forum brings together the minister of Indigenous affairs and northern development along with the Yukon premier and First Nation government leaders. In short, the FNFAs and SGAs are the rules and regulations that now inform Indigenous-state relations in the Yukon.

Self-governing First Nations have their own governing structures. First Nation constitutions establish both the legal and the moral authority to govern in addition to setting out the membership code, governing bodies, and the rights and freedoms of their citizens. While some communities have adopted more liberal democratic institutions and arrangements, others have opted to reintroduce elements of the traditional clan-based system into their governing structures. For example, the Kwanlin Dün First Nation has five separate branches of government: the General Assembly, Elders Council, Youth Council, Judicial Council, and an elected chief and council.[16] The government of the Carcross/Tagish First Nation is structured on a clan system.[17] The constitution of the Ta'an Kwäch'än Council establishes five branches of government, but also recognizes six traditional families and provides for their representation in the General Assembly, the Board of Directors, and the Youth Council.[18] The cultural foundation of Indigenous governance has sparked heated debate in academic and policy circles. As De la Torre (2010, 224) warns us, culture-based political and decision-making processes may not take into account the economic, gender, educational, and power differences among individuals within communities, or the way in which consensus-building approaches may mask coercive mechanisms that punish those who dissent. In the case of the Yukon, however, the citizens of self-governing First Nations are not precluded from asserting their rights as Canadian citizens.

The achievement of First Nation self-government in the Yukon was the first step in the process of Indigenous empowerment. The successful conclusion of the negotiation process brought to the surface the underlying tension within First Nation communities over the demand for local autonomy and the need for a central governing authority. Yukon First Nations have long preferred a more focused, community-specific approach to self-government, as opposed to the incorporation of multiple communities into a single governance structure (Coates and Morrison 2008, 108). In 1990, after the finalization of the UFA, the General Assembly of the Council for Yukon Indians voted to undertake a series of community consultations to determine the future of the organization. First Nation communities were clear in their message that self-government authorities were to rest with each First Nation. The consultations led to the downsizing and restructuring of the CYI. The chair was reappointed on a temporary basis and the four vice-chair positions were eliminated. A special meeting of the General Assembly in 1994 produced even more resolutions to downsize the organization and transfer much of its power and resources to the individual First Nation governments. The membership felt that a large and powerful central body would stifle the local exercise of power (CYFN 2005, 8). The CYI was reconstituted by its membership as a land claims implementation office. While the achievement of self-government required First Nations to create a collective political identity, their success allowed them to unbundle this political unity in a way that would lead to their emancipation.

In 1995, the CYI reclaimed its role as a political advocacy organization. A new constitution was drafted and put before the General Assembly. The constitution proposed that the organization be renamed the Council of Yukon

First Nations (CYFN). It also advanced a bold new organizational vision. The CYFN would become a governing body whose power and authority would be derived from those of its members (CYFN 2010). In other words, based on its delegated authority, the CYFN would enjoy a government-to-government relationship with the federal and territorial governments.[19] The political structure of the CYFN was reorganized around the office of the grand chief, who would be elected by the members of the General Assembly for a three-year term to act as the leader and spokesperson for the organization. Eleven of the Yukon's fourteen First Nations accepted and signed the new constitution. Three First Nations refused to become members of the CYFN: the Kwanlin Dün First Nation, Liard First Nation, and the Ross River Dena Council. The Kwanlin Dün First Nation has assumed its own political representational role, while the Liard First Nation and the Ross River Dena Council generally seek representation through the Kaska Dena Council, a body that advances the interests of the Kaska Dena people (MacDonald 2005). More recently, the Vuntut Gwitchin First Nation decided to withdraw from the CYFN, with a representative from the Vuntut Gwitchin First Nation Government stating that "They [CYFN] have nothing to offer us. Vuntut is a self-governing nation. We can do things on our own."[20] At times, the CYFN coordinates with the Yukon government in matters pertaining to the implementation of the UFA. It also acts as an ambassador, representing the Yukon First Nations at the national and international levels.

Party politics is a prominent feature of life in the Yukon. In contrast to Nunavut and the Northwest Territories, where territorial governments follow a more traditional structure of governance that precludes political parties, the Yukon has a parliamentary system with three major parties and a vigorous form of responsible government (Alcantara 2013). According to Darius Elias, a First Nation member of the Legislative Assembly (MLA) for the Liberal Party, in his community of Old Crow, as in much of the Yukon, Indigenous voters tend to vote for the person, not the party.[21] Ongoing tensions between the self-governing First Nations and the Yukon government over such issues as the provision of social services, land-use planning and consultation, and resource and power sharing has drawn Yukon First Nations into territorial party politics. As Grand Chief Ruth Massie of the CYFN has noted, the implementation of land claims and self-government agreements is aided by having Indigenous people and their allies in the Yukon Legislative Assembly.[22] Given the small population sizes of and large geographic distances between communities in the Yukon, it is clear that neither the First Nation governments nor the territorial government has the resources or the capacity to provide programs and services on their own (Cameron and White 1995, 33). For the foreseeable future, the advancement of First Nation autonomy and self-government in the Yukon depends on a productive interplay between Indigenous and public governments.

## Conclusion

This chapter has attempted to explain how Yukon First Nations achieved an important measure of autonomy and self-government through the comprehensive land claims process. Conventional explanations have emphasized the favourable political and legal context, the availability of institutional allies, and the geographic remoteness of the First Nation communities involved as key factors in the successful negotiation process. In addition to these structural and institutional factors, I have suggested that the actors themselves made a difference to the outcome through their strategy of interest representation. The strength of the Yukon First Nations has been their collective political voice and vision with respect to the demand for territory and autonomy. The Council for Yukon Indians played a central role in relaying this message to the federal government. It worked to create a strong collective political identity that would further First Nation interests in the negotiation process without undermining community-specific goals and priorities. Important democratic outcomes of the twenty-year negotiation process include persuading the federal government to shift its policy to better accommodate the needs of the Yukon First Nations in such areas as subsurface land rights and in obtaining the model of self-government envisioned by the communities (CYFN 2005). The CYI accomplished its mandate. It has been an effective mediator on behalf of First Nation communities. Nevertheless, its capacity to unify the interests of the Yukon's fourteen First Nations and to serve as a locus for the centralization of authority has worked against the organization in the post-1995 period. First Nation unity was not intended to come at the expense of individual community interests and identities. The creation of a central authority was always envisioned as a stepping stone along the path to community empowerment.

There is much that can be learned from studying the Yukon case. A principal lesson in the achievement of a nation-to-nation-type relationship between Indigenous peoples and the state is that party politics and Indigenous autonomy can be mutually reinforcing when Indigenous peoples are in positions of power. Indigenous members of the Yukon Legislative Assembly whom I interviewed indicated that they entered politics in part to ensure that the government works to advance the interests of Indigenous peoples and to serve in the implementation of land claim and self-government legislation. A second lesson that can be drawn from this case is the important role that Indigenous ownership and control over surface and subsurface resources play in successful experiments in autonomy and self-government. As outlined by the Yukon chiefs in their visionary plan for land claim and self-government negotiations with Ottawa, *Together Today for Our Children Tomorrow*, both economic and political rights are central for advancing Indigenous agendas. Finally, the Yukon case demonstrates that improving Indigenous-state relations requires trust and a willingness to work together and share responsibilities on the part of Indigenous and settler governments as the former build up their internal governing capacity. There is a new order of government in the Yukon that must be respected by the territorial and federal governments. To conclude with the words of former chief of Carcross/Tagish First Nation, Doris McLean, "I think the best thing that happened to us First Nations of the Yukon was self-government."[23]

# 3

# Bolivia: Advancing Indigenous Governance as a Distinct Order of Government

*Indigenous governments must function for plurinationality to succeed.*

—René Laime Yucen, Vice Ministry of Indigenous Autonomies[1]

Bolivia was the first country in the world to incorporate the 2007 United Nations Declaration on the Rights of Indigenous Peoples into its constitution (Albó 2010; Schilling-Vacaflor and Kuppe 2012). This move was facilitated by Bolivia's constitutional reform process, which aimed to "re-found" the country under the leadership of its first Indigenous-identified president, Evo Morales (2006–19) and his political party, the Movement toward Socialism (MAS). Even though Indigenous peoples constitute the majority of the population in Bolivia (62 per cent), they suffer social, economic, and political exclusion (Retolaza Eguren 2008, 312). Born in 1959 in the agricultural department of Oruro to Aymara parents, Morales grew up in abject poverty. Only two of his six siblings survived past childhood. In 1982, after a devastating drought in the highlands, he and his family relocated to the Quechua-speaking valley region of Cochabamba, where they began to cultivate coca, the principal ingredient used in the production of cocaine. Confronted with US-enforced eradication programs, the growers defended coca production as part of Indigenous culture and traditions. By the 1990s, Morales had become the undisputed leader of the coca growers' movement. In 1999, he and his supporters formed the MAS and successfully competed in municipal elections.

In 2002, he was narrowly defeated in the first round of that year's presidential elections. The ultimate victory for the MAS came during the December 2005 elections, when the party captured 54 per cent of the national vote, the only party to win an absolute majority since the country's transition to democracy in 1982 (Rice 2011a, 277–8).

Now that Indigenous peoples have arrived at the presidency, what Indigenous and democratic governance innovations have been implemented? What lessons and challenges does the case of Bolivia provide about advancing Indigenous rights and representation in new democracies? This chapter suggests that Bolivia constitutes an important example of Indigenous self-government as a third order of government (Abele and Prince 2006), or what Tockman (2006, 154) has termed "a distinctly Bolivian hybrid model of [I]ndigenous autonomy." In a third-order model of Indigenous governance, Indigenous nations "join" the state and its political system. While Indigenous governments may enjoy more power within this system as a result, they are still subordinate to the state (Abele and Prince 2006, 579). Bolivia's 2009 constitution modified virtually every aspect of the Bolivian state in ways favourable to Indigenous peoples, even officially renaming the country the Plurinational State of Bolivia. The new constitution and its secondary laws created more spaces for Indigenous participation and inclusion by establishing three levels of autonomous, non-hierarchical sub-national governments with legislative capacities: departmental, municipal, and Indigenous (Komadina 2016; Zegada and Brockmann Quiroga 2016). Although the model of the state that underpins the new regime remains unitary, the state is gradually shifting in power and practice toward a functioning intercultural democratic form of government that rests on Indigenous autonomy (Exeni Rodríguez 2012; Postero and Tockman 2020). As indicated by the chapter's epigraph—which comes from a unit head in the Vice Ministry of Indigenous Autonomies—the success of Bolivia's experiment in plurinationality is inextricably linked with the strength of its Indigenous governments.

The broadening of democracy to include Indigenous peoples in Bolivia has brought a wider range of political options for Indigenous activists, who no longer face the strategic dilemma of whether or not to push for change from within the institutions of the state. This dynamic, I argue, has had a profoundly democratizing effect on the country's political system and is one of the major advantages of the third-order-of-government approach. In order to trace this development, the chapter unfolds first with an overview of the rise of Bolivia's powerful Indigenous rights movement and its demand for plurinationality. This section details the evolution of the Bolivian political system from a "pacted" democracy to an intercultural one. Following the general trend in Latin America throughout the 1990s, Indigenous movements in Bolivia played a central role in the country's social upheavals. Through the use of parallel or solidarity protest events, Indigenous and popular groups have been effective in shutting down the entire country until their demands are met (Anria 2019; Rice 2012). The chapter then turns to an examination of the new institutional architecture in Bolivia under the governing MAS party. It explores such democratic and Indigenous governance innovations as the creation of special reserved seats in the new Plurinational Legislative Assembly for minority Indigenous nations, the creation of Indigenous autonomies, and the mainstreaming of Indigenous rights throughout all levels of government. The final section of the chapter looks at the challenge of implementing Indigenous rights to autonomy and self-government in the context of state ownership and control over subsurface mineral resources. It does so by examining resource conflicts between highland and lowland Indigenous groups and the state, as well as between the Morales administration and the country's formerly dominant or elite groups (Canessa 2018). The chapter concludes with a discussion of the merits and limits of state efforts at decolonization in Bolivia and the key lessons learned from this case study.

## Plurinationality and the Indigenous Movement

Bolivia is a small, landlocked country of 12.22 million inhabitants (as of 2022) in the heart of South America. With a per capita gross domestic product of just US$3,143 in 2020, it is one of the poorest countries in the Western Hemisphere.[2] Bolivia is the only country in South America with a majority Indigenous population. The Andean mountain range dominates the Bolivian landscape, dividing the country into the windswept highlands, or *altiplano*, and the tropical Amazonian lowlands. The country's dominant Indigenous groups are the Aymara people of the highland plateau region and the Quechua people of the highland valley region. In the Bolivian lowlands, there are over thirty minority Indigenous groups, including the Guaraní, Chiquitano, and Mojeño peoples (Canessa 2018; Lucero 2008). Organized resistance by the populace has long been a part of the country's politics—culminating in the Bolivian National Revolution of 1952. Throughout much of the twentieth century, the militant labour movement that grew out of Bolivia's mineral export economy was a major actor in the political life of the nation (Collier and Collier 2002; Rueschemeyer, Stephens, and Stephens 1992). The neoliberal-inspired "shock therapy" program of 1985 dramatically curtailed the power of organized labour. The consolidation of market reforms in the 1990s further demobilized civil society (Conaghan and Malloy 1994). The late 1990s, however, saw a dramatic surge in protest activity on the part of new social and political actors, most notably Indigenous peoples, that ultimately led to the unravelling of the neoliberal economic model and the search for new avenues of participation and inclusion for those traditionally marginalized in Bolivian democracy (Rice 2012).

Bolivia, like much of Latin America, has long suffered from exclusionary governing structures. Political parties in Bolivia have generally served more as vehicles for the capture and circulation of state patronage among political elites than as organizations expressing the interests of society (Gamarra and Malloy 1995). Bolivia's neoliberal governments of the 1980s and '90s relied heavily on political pacts between the major parties to impose draconian structural adjustment programs. Shortly after launching his New Economic Policy (NEP) in 1985, President Víctor Paz Estenssoro of the National Revolutionary Movement (Movimiento Nacional Revolucionario, or MNR) negotiated the so-called Pact for Democracy. The pact provided legislative support for the new policy in exchange for a share of state patronage for the main opposition party, the National Democratic Action (Acción Democrática Nacionalista, or ADN) led by former dictator Hugo Bánzer Suárez, as well as a mechanism to ensure the rotation of the presidency between the two parties (Gamarra 1994). Defenders of the pact argued that since the arrangement was between the top two finishers in the presidential elections, then a majority of the electorate was duly represented. However, the opposition, headed by Jamie Paz Zamora of the Movement of the Revolutionary Left (Movimiento de la Izquierda Revolucionaria, or MIR) charged the two leaders with attempting to establish a hegemonic party. In a round of political bargaining, the MIR's electoral reform proposal favouring minority parties was accepted in exchange for the official opposition's mild resistance to the NEP. Together, the MNR, ADN, and MIR coalitions came to dominate elections throughout the 1990s, rotating in and out of power. While the ability to form coalitions gave the party system a measure of stability, it also effectively shut out non-coalition parties from access to the state. As a result, Bolivia's pacted democracy generated the potential for frustrated opposition groups to resort to extra-systemic means of affecting change (Rice 2011a).

In an attempt to draw in excluded sectors of the polity, the government of President Gonzalo Sánchez de Lozada of the MNR undertook a number of important electoral reforms in the mid-1990s. A key reform initiative was the 1994 Ley de Participación Popular (Law of Popular Participation, LPP), which was one of several new pieces of legislation designed to incorporate increasingly mobilized Indigenous peoples into the legal and political life of the country (Kohl 2002; Postero 2007). The reforms served the dual goal of cutting back on the central government's expenses and responsibilities by downloading them to the local level while co-opting resistance to neoliberalism by shifting the focus of popular struggles to local issues rather than national ones (Arce and Rice 2009; Veltmeyer 2007). The LPP instituted the first-ever direct municipal elections, significantly strengthened local governments, and provided Indigenous organizations with key powers of municipal oversight. The newly created oversight committees sought to formalize traditional Indigenous institutions and include them in the political system through a top-down process of controlled inclusion. Although the LPP was not based on a model of citizenship as agency, the reforms had a number of unanticipated benefits. In addition to creating opportunities for the emergence of local political systems, the reforms aided in the development of new local leaders and movements, including Evo Morales and the MAS (Laserna 2002). The more favourable set of institutional opportunities led to a shift in strategy on the part of Bolivia's Indigenous and popular movements from direct action tactics to electoral competition. According to Gutiérrez Rojas (2003, 184), the presidential elections of 2002, which the MAS lost by a narrow margin, were historic in that they marked the first time in Bolivian history that Indigenous peoples voted for Indigenous candidates.

The MAS managed to project itself onto the national political stage during a period of social mobilization in the early 2000s by moving the focus of resistance beyond the local level to a national critique of the neoliberal economic model and of a political system that produced strong barriers to genuine participation. The victorious Water War of Cochabamba in 2000 against the privatization of that city's water supply marked the first in a series of massive civil uprisings that led to a rupture in the national political system and the dissolution of the neoliberal consensus (Kohl and Farthing 2006; Olivera and Lewis 2004). The period of social mobilization reached its peak with the Gas War in the capital city of La Paz in October 2003, which led to the ouster of President Sánchez de Lozada, who was then in office for a second time. The underlying factors in the mass mobilization included the social costs of economic restructuring, the control of strategic sectors of the economy by transnational capital, and the loss of legitimacy on the part of the nation's democratic institutions (Bonifaz 2004; Suárez 2003). The crisis highlighted the complete disconnect between the state and society. The protest cycle ultimately opened the door to Morales's presidential victory. As noted by Exeni Rodríguez (2012, 222), "One of the fundamental lessons of Bolivian political culture is that the most creative democratic moments occur through extrainstitutional mobilization. Important adjustments and expansions in institutions cannot be explained without this 'politics in the streets.' " Levitsky and Roberts (2011, 408) have suggested that Morales was not only a political outsider, but a regime outsider who won on a pledge to abolish the established political order and re-establish the country along more inclusive, participatory lines.

The 2005 presidential win by Morales and the MAS marked the end of Bolivia's neoliberal state and its pacted form of democracy. The 2009 constitution became the tool used to transform the state. Indigenous and popular-sector input was central to the democratic gains secured in the new constitution. The publicly elected constituent assembly that drafted the document counted on the active participation of civil society organizations, political parties, and governing officials. Among the representatives elected to the constituent assembly, 55.8 per cent self-identified as Indigenous (Sieder and Barrera Vivero 2017, 11). In a concerted effort to influence the direction of the new constitution, Bolivia's main Indigenous and peasant organizations came together as part of the so-called Unity Pact to draft their own proposal (Zegada et al. 2011; Tapia 2011).[3] The document put forward by the Unity Pact introduced the concepts of communitarian democracy, decolonization, plurinationality, and Indigenous autonomy, which were subsequently taken up by the MAS and incorporated in the new constitutional text, albeit in reduced form. The Unity Pact member organizations envisioned a form of democracy in which Indigenous communities would govern themselves at the local level while being actively involved in national decision-making processes, particularly with regard to the development of natural resources within their territories (Hilborn 2014). Plurinationality, a key demand of the Indigenous movement, recognizes the plurality of nations within a state (Tockman 2017). It replaces, at least conceptually, the unidirectional relationship between the state and Indigenous groups with a bilateral or government-to-government relationship based on mutual respect and consideration (Becker 2011; Walsh 2009). Tapia (2011) has suggested that the Unity Pact served as the space for imagining and designing a plurinational state, while the MAS was tasked with narrowing it to fit within the confines of a liberal state.

## Indigenous and Democratic Governance Innovations

The MAS is the most successful Indigenous-based political party in Bolivia's history.[4] In its first electoral outing, in the 1999 municipal elections, the MAS captured 11 mayoral victories, 8 of which were in the department of Cochabamba. By the national elections of 2002, the MAS had greatly increased its support base, garnering 21 per cent of the national vote and winning 27 seats in the legislature and 8 seats in the senate (Van Cott 2005, 86). In 2005, the MAS took many political analysts by surprise when it captured a majority share of the presidential vote (54 per cent). Following the 2005 elections, the MAS held a majority of seats in the legislature, with 72 out of 130 lower-house seats going to the party. However, the MAS narrowly missed winning a majority in the senate when it secured only 12 out of the 27 seats (Gamarra 2008). Morales and the MAS won another convincing victory in the presidential elections of December 2009, garnering 64 per cent of the vote. This time, the MAS won a two-thirds majority in both the national legislature and the senate. In 2014, Morales was elected to a third term (technically, his second term under the rules of the new constitution) with 61 per cent of the vote. In 2019, Morales made a disastrous attempt to run for a fourth presidential term. Disputes over the transparency and legitimacy of the vote led to a political crisis and the call for new elections. In the 2020 elections, the MAS made a stunning comeback, garnering 55 per cent of the vote under the new leadership of Morales's hand-picked successor, former minister of the economy and public finance Luis Arce (Phillips and Collyns 2020). The majority of Indigenous representatives in Bolivia have gained office through the governing MAS party. Whereas only four Indigenous representatives held legislative seats during the heyday of Bolivia's "pacted" democracy of the late 1980s and early 1990s, today there are over forty Indigenous representatives in the legislature (see table 3.1).

**Table 3.1** Indigenous legislators in Bolivia (lower and upper houses), 1989–2020

| Session | Total number of seats | Number of Indigenous legislators | % of Indigenous legislators |
|---|---|---|---|
| National Congress, 1989–93 | 157 | 4 | 2.5 |
| National Congress, 1993–7 | 157 | 6 | 3.8 |
| National Congress, 2005–9 | 157 | 27 | 17.2 |
| Plurinational Legislative Assembly, 2009–14* | 166 | 43 | 25.9 |
| Plurinational Legislative Assembly, 2020–* | 166 | 42 | 25.3 |

*Sources*: Loayza Bueno (2012, 8) and current legislator profiles, available at https://diputados.gob.bo/diputados-home/ and https://web.senado.gob.bo/legislativa/bancadas.
*Total number of seats includes the 7 reserved seats for Indigenous representatives.

To ensure the direct participation of minority Indigenous groups in the political system, the MAS created a small number of reserved seats in the legislature for Indigenous members (Barié 2020). The 2009 Transitory Electoral Regime Law established special non-contiguous Indigenous circumscriptions for minority Indigenous nations in seven of Bolivia's nine departments (see table 4.2). The departments of Chuquisaca and Potosí do not qualify for Indigenous circumscriptions given that their Indigenous populations are predominantly from the Quechua nation, one of two majority Indigenous nations who reside in the western highlands (Komadina 2016, 8). Afro-Bolivians, who make up a tiny proportion of the total population (less than 1 per cent) and are classified as "Indigenous" by the Bolivian government, are included in the special Indigenous circumscriptions (Htun and Ossa 2013). Were it not for these special circumscriptions, smaller Indigenous groups, especially in the eastern lowlands, would not be able to count on legislative representation. The lists of candidates for the Indigenous circumscriptions are elaborated according to traditional norms, customs, and procedures—ensuring an organic and direct relationship between representatives and constituents—but must respect the gender-parity legislation put into place by the Morales government in 2010 (Fuentes and Sánchez 2018).[5] Voters within Indigenous circumscriptions have the option of choosing either the special ballot for Indigenous candidates or the regular ballot for their district.

**Table 3.2** Bolivia's lower house legislative circumscriptions and eligibility by department, 2020 general elections

| Department | Special Indigenous reserved seats | Eligible groups per reserved seat |
|---|---|---|
| Beni | 1 | Tacana; Pacahuara; Itonama; Joaquiniano; Maropa; Guarasgwe; Mojeño; Sirionó; Baure; Tsimane; Movima; Cayubaba; Moré; Cavineño; Chacobo; Canichana; Mosetén; Yuracaré |
| Chuquisaca | 0 | None—majority Indigenous nations |
| Cochabamba | 1 | Yuracaré; Yuqui |
| La Paz | 1 | Afro-Bolivians; Mosetén; Leco; Kallawaya; Tacana; Araona |
| Oruro | 1 | Chipaya; Uru Murato |
| Pando | 1 | Yaminagua; Pacahuara; Esse Ejja; Machineri; Tacana |
| Potosí | 0 | None—majority Indigenous nations |
| Santa Cruz | 1 | Chiquitano; Guaraní; Guarayo; Ayoreo; Yuracaré; Mojeño |
| Tarija | 1 | Guaraní; Weenayek; Tapíete |

*Source*: "Atlas electoral de Bolivia, Gestión 2021 v3.0.0," Órgano Electoral Plurinacional, accessed January 14, 2024, https://atlaselectoral.oep.org.bo/#/.

The MAS's efforts at creating an "intercultural" democracy have resulted in the expansion of representation for marginalized groups in Bolivian society. Intercultural democracy is defined in the 2009 constitution (article 11) as a direct and participatory, representative, and communal form of government. The constitutional recognition of communitarian democracy holds considerable promise as a means to strengthen democratic governance by constructively linking formal and non-formal or non-state institutions (Retolaza Eguren 2008). The creation of self-governing Indigenous bodies is key to fostering communitarian democracy, and ultimately, to the realization of the plurinational state. According to Cameron and Sharpe (2012, 246), "The cumulative effect of these innovations is to use direct institutionalized voice to transform and democratize the state as a whole—not by scaling up but by devolving more democratic power to small-scale self-governing communities everywhere." Under the current constitutional configuration, communitarian democracy is relegated to lower-level governments—it is to be exercised within Indigenous communities through the election or selection of governing authorities using traditional methods. However, as Zegada et al. (2011) point out, the electoral methods and governance structures at the local level do not inform practices at the national level. Nonetheless, these constitutional gains are an important step in building an authentic intercultural democracy.

What we are witnessing in Bolivia today is the "hybridization" of the institutions of representative democracy with elements from the participatory democratic tradition as well as from Indigenous governance practices that seems to serve the populace well (Komadina 2016, 3). In Anria's (2016, 103) estimation, "Indigenous peoples do enjoy increased access to the state. They are better able to influence decision making, and can be found in representative institutions at all levels of government. They are included, therefore, not only as voters, but as makers of policy." Racism and patriarchy have been identified by the Morales administration as the two underpinnings of the colonial state that need to be uprooted before the plurinational state can take hold. Whereas the concept of decolonization refers to the revalorization, recognition, and re-establishment of Indigenous cultures, traditions, and values within the institutions that govern society, de-patriarchalization is understood as the process of removing male privilege from these institutions (Vice Ministerio de Descolonización 2013). Both decolonization and de-patriarchalization enhance democratic representation by bringing Indigenous and women's voices into the political process, thereby reorienting public policy toward society's most vulnerable members while expanding the nature of public debate (Eversole 2010; Peruzzotti and Selee 2009). The new spaces of citizen engagement in Bolivia are construed less as an alternative to democracy than as part of an effort to overcome the basic problems associated with representative democracy (Exeni Rodríguez 2012).

To advance the restructuring of the state, the Morales administration created new institutional interfaces between the state and society. The introduction of a number of bold and innovative vice ministries in 2009 was the first step in generating strategic projects, programs, and policies to mainstream Indigenous rights throughout the governing apparatus. Chief among them were the Vice Ministry of Indigenous Justice, the Vice Ministry of Traditional Health, the Vice Ministry of Intercultural Education, the Vice Ministry of Decolonization, the Vice Ministry of Indigenous Autonomies, and the Vice Ministry of Coordination with Social Movements and Civil Society (Rice 2016). Beginning in 2017, the government restructured many of these vice ministries. For instance, the Ministry of Autonomies, which was home to the Vice Ministry of Indigenous Autonomies, was itself downgraded to a vice ministry within the Ministry of the Presidency (Tockman 2017). This move may have been prompted by the growing tension between the MAS and its pursuit of centralized control over the state and the desire of Indigenous communities for greater autonomy from the state (Cameron and Plata 2021; Postero and Tockman 2020). Yet, the Vice Ministry of Decolonization, which was previously housed within the Ministry of Cultures and Tourism, has since been upgraded to the Ministry of Cultures, Decolonization, and Depatriarchalization under the administration of President Arce. The MAS continues to cast itself as a "government of social movements" by appointing the leaders of such movements to government posts as part of its effort to "lead by obeying" (Zegada et al. 2011, 243). More than two-thirds of the deputies in the national legislature now share this background (García Linera 2014, 51). For the first time in Bolivian history, the government closely resembles and reflects its citizens.

The Morales administration considered government bureaucracy to be the main impediment to the implementation of its policies and programs. According to the vice minister of decolonization (2014, 116), "much of our effort will be wasted if there are entities and public authorities within our system that are producing neo-colonization by way of the rules and norms of previous administrations, and so we must remedy this by issuing new standards that give life to the plurinational state." The government passed a number of laws to enhance civil and political rights in the country. For example, the 2010 Anti-racism and Anti-discrimination Law authorizes criminal sanctions against public- and private-sector institutions, including those of the media, that disseminate racist and biased ideas (Farthing and Kohl 2014, 65). In 2012, a Language Rights Law was passed requiring all public and private institutions serving the public to have their staff trained in the official Indigenous languages of use in the regions in which they are located (*Gaceta Oficial del Estado Plurinacional de Bolivia* 2012). An empirical study of the extent of bureaucratic decolonization in Bolivia compared the profiles of civil servants from 2001 and 2013 and found the public administrative body of today to be younger, with a greater presence of women, and a record number of Indigenous people. An impressive 48 per cent of public employees now self-identify as Indigenous (Soruco Sologuren, Franco Pinto, and Durán Azurduy 2014, 14). These findings suggest that broad-based changes are occurring within the government.

Bolivia's latest experiment with decentralization offers the best hope of bringing about a fundamental restructuring of Indigenous-state relations by the way in which it devolves power to local Indigenous communities. The 2010 Framework Law of Autonomy and Decentralization regulates the new territorial organization of the state as defined in the 2009 constitution. In addition to the recognition of the three levels of sub-national governments in Bolivia (departmental, regional, and municipal), the constitution also identifies Indigenous autonomies as a separate and distinct order of government, one that is not directly subordinate to the other levels (CIPCA 2009; Herrera Acuña 2021). Under current provisions, existing Indigenous territories as well as municipalities and regions with a substantial Indigenous presence may convert themselves into self-governing entities—known as Indigenous First Peoples Peasant Autonomies (Autonomías Indígenas Originarias Campesinas, or AIOCs)—based on traditional norms, customs, institutions, and authorities (Faguet 2014). The constitutional provision that AIOCs may join together to form larger territorial units if so desired ensures that Indigenous autonomy is not limited to the municipal level (González 2015). To convert to an AIOC, jurisdictions must successfully complete a number of state-imposed requirements, including holding a referendum among residents and developing autonomy statutes that must be approved by the state. An analysis of draft autonomy statutes carried out by Tockman, Cameron, and Plata (2015) revealed significant variation among AIOCs, with some having more communitarian designs of self-governance and others with more municipal structures of liberal design. Perhaps most telling, out of a total of twenty-two jurisdictions that initiated a process to AIOC conversion, only two municipalities (Charagua Iyambae and Uru Chipaya) and one Indigenous territory (Raqaypampa) have so far succeeded in becoming formally recognized self-governing Indigenous autonomies (Cameron and Plata 2021, 152).

Once established, AIOCs are afforded a wide range of governing authorities, including the administration of taxes, the management of renewable natural resources, the development of economic and social programs and policies, and the exercise of traditional justice (Barrera 2012; Tockman 2006). In 2015, the municipality of Charagua Iyambae, in the lowland department of Santa Cruz, became Bolivia's first AIOC after its majority Guaraní population approved its conversion. Postero and Tockman's (2020) analysis of the first three years of Charagua Iyambae's functioning as an Indigenous autonomy revealed that while the question of non-renewable natural resource extraction continues to undermine the realization of full self-determination, Indigenous norms and practices are being exercised in significant and meaningful ways by the new government. In their estimation,

> While there are ongoing contestations that will need to be sorted out, Charagua Iyambae appears to be a functioning intercultural democratic form of government. By this we mean that the system in place allows the possibility of constructive political relations between Indigenous and non-Indigenous residents, who are treated as equals. Each sector is recognized according to its political culture; given voice, rights, and obligations; and has the opportunity to participate in direct deliberative processes. (2020, 12)

The example of Charagua Iyambae illustrates the possibilities and constraints of embedding or nesting Indigenous autonomy and self-government within the liberal framework of the nation-state as a distinct order of government.

## Indigenous Rights and Resource Conflicts

The governance innovations of the MAS have brought about important changes to the structure of the state, the practise of democracy, and the national identity of Bolivia. Yet, in practice, tensions and contradictions within the new constitution itself have limited the construction of the plurinational state. According to constitutional scholar Roberto Gargarella (2013), a highly centralized organization of power tends to work against the application of Indigenous rights. Bolivia's new constitution concentrates state power while expanding Indigenous rights. Stated differently, it pits governance against government. For instance, the Morales government's commitment to Indigenous autonomy was at odds with its resource-dependent, state-led model of development. The constitutional provision that all non-renewable resources remain under state control places firm limits on the right to autonomy and self-government (Tockman and Cameron 2014). Article 30.15 of the constitution establishes the right of Indigenous peoples to free, prior, and informed consultation—not consent—concerning planned measures affecting them, such as mining and oil or gas exploration. The constitution does stipulate that the state must conduct the prior consultation process in good faith and in a concerted fashion, and that it should respect local Indigenous norms and procedures. Nevertheless, Indigenous groups cannot veto state-sponsored development and resource-extraction projects in their territories (Schilling-Vacaflor and Kuppe 2012; Wolff 2012). As it stands, the new constitution does not fully change power relations between the state and Indigenous peoples.

The gap between discourse and practice in contemporary Bolivia is also apparent in the MAS's approach to the idea of "Living Well." The new constitution makes an explicit commitment to the rights of Nature and to the Andean Indigenous principle of Living Well (*Vivir Bien* in Spanish; *Sumac Kawsay* in Quechua; *Suma Qamaña* in Aymara) as an alternative model of development around which the state and its policies should be organized (Bretón, Cortez, and García 2014; Ugalde 2014). An examination of Bolivia's National Development Plan (2016–20), however, reveals the gap between the government's official discourse on Living Well, for instance, and its conventional strategy for economic development on the basis of natural resource wealth.[6] The term "development" appears four times more frequently in the government's planning document than that of "Living Well," and forty times more frequently than the reference to Indigenous autonomy. The Living Well principle is based on the value of living well with others (as opposed to living better than others), including non-human beings and the natural world (Fischer and Fasol 2013). It represents an alternative to Western conceptualizations of development based on higher material standards of living. The concept of Living Well plays an important role in building consensus among Indigenous and environmental activists, as well as the broader public, for the MAS's agenda for change. The National Development Plan utilizes Bolivia's inferior position in the global economy as well as the capture of the state by elites to justify the government's incursion into Indigenous territories to extract natural resource wealth in order to achieve the long-term goal of Living Well for all of its citizens (Plan de Desarrollo Económico y Social 2016, 1).

The tensions between neo-extractivist development and Indigenous autonomy reached a peak during Bolivia's infamous highway conflict. In August 2011, violence erupted in the lowland department of Beni over the government's proposed highway project through the Isiboro Sécure Indigenous Territory and National Park (Territorio Indígena y Parque Nacional Isiboro-Sécure, or TIPNIS). The MAS maintained that the proposed Villa Tunari–San Ignacio de Moxos highway was essential for national development as it would connect the central Andean highlands with the lowlands to the north.

The local residents balked at the government's lack of prior consultation over the proposal, as stipulated in the new constitution (AIN 2011). Prior consultation is a democratic innovation that facilitates deliberation and decision making in the extractives sector (Exeni Rodríguez 2012). In response, the government passed the Law of Prior Consultation on February 10, 2012, to begin the process of community consultation in the TIPNIS to decide if the highway project should proceed. Between July 29 and December 7, 2012, the government reached out to all 69 resident communities. According to official data, 55 communities agreed to support the road, 3 opposed it, and 11 boycotted the process ("TSE: Los Indígenas Aceptan" 2013). Although the government garnered 80 per cent support for the project, it did not achieve consensus within the Indigenous communities or gain the backing of the TIPNIS Sub-central, the main Indigenous authority in the zone (Achtenberg 2012). On April 25, 2013, amid vows to impede the highway's construction from opposition groups, Morales cancelled the project (Rice 2014b). The TIPNIS controversy revealed the importance of social mobilization around the contradictions in constitutional texts and official discourse as a means to sway government policy in favour of Indigenous rights and as a continuing check on state power in Bolivia.

The MAS administration has also faced significant opposition from formerly dominant actors who now find themselves excluded from the state. Morales's rise to power polarized the country into regional camps. On the one hand, regional elites centered in the eastern lowland departments desire a lean, neoliberal state that eschews centralism in favour of regional authority. They claim that the central government discriminates against white and *mestizo* (mixed race) people by only representing the interests of Indigenous and poor people (Eaton 2007; Fabricant 2009; Gustafson 2008). On the other hand, government supporters based largely in the western highland departments back a strong centralized, interventionist, and redistributive state. The result is a highly politicized regional cleavage with racial and class overtones. However, as Madrid (2012, 165) points out, the polarization between supporters and opponents of the MAS government is more ideological and regional than ethnic in nature. Opposition groups in the eastern lowland departments have resolved not to recognize the new constitution, and instead agitate for greater regional autonomy. Having lost their voice in the political system, the regional elites are looking for an exit (Eaton 2007).

## Conclusion

Bolivia has the most advanced and comprehensive Indigenous rights regime of any country in Latin America (González 2015). This chapter has analyzed the democratic and Indigenous governance innovations implemented by the administration of President Evo Morales of the governing MAS party. I have suggested that the exercise of Indigenous autonomy and self-government in Bolivia reflects a third-order-of-government approach that implies a "root and branch reform" of the entire system as Indigenous governments become intermeshed with the established political order (Abele and Prince 2006, 586). Indigenous participation in decision-making bodies from the local to the national levels enables Indigenous communities to have a say in the policies that affect their lives both directly and indirectly (Tomaselli 2017). The Bolivian case indicates that new types of institutions need to be created or recognized as part of the political framework if Indigenous peoples are to realize a measure of self-determination within the institutional contexts and state structures in which they live (Eversole 2010). Scholars of Indigenous politics have pointed out that Bolivia represents a "distinct" form of Indigenous autonomy in Latin America (e.g., Postero 2017; Tockman 2006; Tockman, Cameron, and Plata 2015). In my interview with the vice minister of decolonization, Félix Cárdenas, he was adamant that Bolivia is not interested in copying models or approaches to autonomy and self-government that are being pursued elsewhere. In his words, "we are charting our own course."[7]

Bolivia's distinctive hybrid or nested model of Indigenous autonomy offers valuable lessons about using liberal state mechanisms to advance the project of decolonization. First and foremost, the Bolivian case suggests that representation and direct action are not mutually exclusive. Bolivia's intercultural democratic form of government came about through popular mobilization, which was in turn channelled into the political system by the MAS (Anria 2019; Rice 2012). Protest broadens and expands democracy by including new actors, issues, and agendas. Secondly, this case instructs us that building unity in diversity requires institutions that are both culturally appropriate and shared. Indigenous people in Bolivia are demographically superior, and yet, until recently, they have been structurally excluded from the state (Retolaza Eguren 2008). By questioning the institutional arrangements that govern them, Indigenous movements have revealed important insights into the cultural basis of formal or state institutions. Yet, formal institutional change is only part of the recipe for improving opportunities for Indigenous peoples and decolonizing democracy—non-state or non-formal institutions also matter to political outcomes (Eversole 2010). Lastly, and relatedly, the practise of Indigenous autonomy and self-government in Bolivia demonstrates the degree to which Indigenous institutions can bolster state institutions and make them more inclusive and participatory. In contemporary Bolivia, representation and participation occurs beyond, and even outside of, political parties (Exeni Rodríguez 2012). This reality requires the recognition and acceptance of new political subjects, such as Indigenous people, in the political sphere. To conclude with the words of Hilda Reinaga, niece of Bolivia's pre-eminent Indigenous writer and intellectual, Fausto Reinaga (1906–94), "Now that we have arrived at the presidency, we will never leave!"[8]

# 4

# Nunavut: Enacting Public Government as Indigenous Self-Government

*What is distinct about the Government of Nunavut is that its vision came from the grassroots.*

> —John Amagoalik, chief commissioner of the
> Nunavut Implementation Commission[1]

On April 1, 1999, Inuit hopes and dreams for a homeland became reality with the creation of Nunavut. Nunavut—which means "our land" in the Inuktitut language—changed the map of Canada through peaceful negotiation and compromise. John Amagoalik, quoted at the top of this chapter, is widely recognized throughout the new territory as the "Father of Nunavut." Although Amagoalik eschews this title—suggesting that the achievement of Nunavut was a collective endeavour—he did play a critical role as a negotiator for the largest land claim settlement in Canadian history and in the design of the new territorial government. His story, and that of Inuit in general,[2] is one of courage and conviction. He provides us with an important example of how activists can achieve a positive outcome when engaging with democratic institutions and processes. Nunavut was a vision of the Inuit communities, and the organizational efforts of Inuit leaders made it a reality. Indigenous peoples around the globe are faced with the dilemma of whether to adopt an oppositional stance to state-imposed political systems, or to try and bring about change by way of the institutional mechanisms such systems offer. As the case of Nunavut demonstrates, autonomy and participation do not have to be mutually exclusive. Inuit have historically been more willing to participate in Canadian political institutions than their southern counterparts (Alcantara 2013; Cairns 2000). By engaging with institutions of the state, Inuit leaders realized the goal of autonomy. Nunavut is the first large-scale test of Indigenous governance in the Americas. The difficult task that now lies ahead for Inuit leaders and their allies is to make this bold experiment work.

This chapter is guided by two central questions: Why did Inuit communities opt for a public government model of Indigenous autonomy and self-government? And what are the major successes, failures, and lessons learned from efforts in Nunavut to incorporate Indigenous values, perspectives, and world views into an established democratic state? I find that Inuit of the eastern Arctic settled on a public government system, as opposed to an Inuit-specific model of self-government, as a means to achieve both economic and political self-determination. The demand for a comprehensive land claims settlement was coupled with the call for the creation of Nunavut for this very reason (Henderson 2009). This model works to advance Indigenous autonomy and self-government in this case due to the relative homogeneity of the majority Inuit population (who form more than 80 per cent of the total territorial population), which ensures their effective control over the entire territory (Cameron and White 1995, 90). At its core, Nunavut is the outcome of a political agreement between an Indigenous people and the federal government of Canada. As a public government model of Indigenous self-government, Nunavut constrains Inuit to work within the established boundaries of state sovereignty while providing them with a measure of power within the state (Abele and Prince 2006; Altamirano-Jiménez 2013). During the negotiation process, Inuit leaders positioned Inuit as a nation within the Canadian state while emphasizing their inherent rights as an Indigenous people (Wilson 2005). The experience of Nunavut can be viewed as part of an ongoing discussion over how Indigenous rights and representation can be formulated and integrated with liberal institutions of democratic government.

The chapter begins with a historical overview of Indigenous-state relations in the eastern Arctic and the events that led up to Inuit demands for the settlement of a comprehensive land claim. This section details the intricacies of negotiating the claim and the task of creating a new Canadian territory. The next section examines the institutional architecture of the new territorial government and its policy and program initiatives as it attempts to meld public and Indigenous self-government regimes. Special attention is paid in this section to the concept of *Inuit Qaujimajatuqangit*—or "that which has long been known by Inuit"—and the Government of Nunavut's struggles to incorporate Indigenous knowledge and perspectives into the structure and function of its operations (Tester and Irniq 2008; Timpson 2009a; White 2006). Given the importance of economic development for political autonomy, the chapter then turns to the pressing issue of how to reconcile Indigenous rights with extractive industry, with a focus on the subsurface mineral rights that were negotiated as part of the comprehensive land claims agreement. The chapter concludes with a discussion of the accomplishments and setbacks that have resulted from the effort to do government differently in Nunavut.

## Negotiating the Claim

The 1993 Nunavut Land Claims Agreement (NLCA) between the Tunngavik Federation of Nunavut (TFN), the Canadian federal government, and the territorial government of the Northwest Territories (NWT) radically restructured Indigenous-state relations in the eastern Arctic. The land claims settlement was an attempt by Inuit to reassert control over their lives and lands in the face of repeated threats from the state. Beginning in the 1950s, Inuit groups in the Canadian Arctic were moved off the land and relocated to government-built settlements in an attempt to change their nomadic way of life and to open up their vast territories to large-scale resource-development projects (Altamirano-Jiménez 2013). In reference to this forced relocation, Tester and Irniq (2008, 57) suggest that "the disruptions to Inuit life and culture were incalculable." Other Inuit families, including that of John Amagoalik, who had been living in northern Quebec, were relocated to the High Arctic region, more than 1,200 kilometres to the north, to act as "human flagpoles" in a Cold War dispute over Arctic sovereignty. The government abandoned these families in a hostile and unfamiliar environment, leaving many to die from exposure and starvation, including many of Amagoalik's friends and family members (McComber 2007). It was not until 2010, due in large part to the tireless efforts of Amagoalik and other High Arctic exiles, that the Government of Canada issued a formal apology to the families for their inhumane treatment and the suffering caused by their relocation (George 2010). Amagoalik grew up in government-run Indian residential schools in Resolute Bay, Churchill, and Frobisher Bay (now Iqaluit). It was in the residential school system where he befriended other future Inuit leaders. Together, this same group of students would later call for the creation of Nunavut.[3]

In 1971, the Inuit Tapirisat of Canada (ITC) was formed as an umbrella organization to represent Inuit voices and interests across the country (see table 4.1). The ITC was the outcome of a national conference organized by Inuit leaders and intellectuals held at Carleton University in Ottawa to discuss how to unify Inuit and coordinate a response to ongoing threats to land rights and social justice in the Arctic (McElroy 2008). Tagak Curley, then the executive secretary of the Indian-Eskimo Association of Canada, served as a conference coordinator, and would go on to become the founder and first president of the ITC. According to Curley, as ITC president he crisscrossed the North gauging public support for the development of a proposal for an Inuit land claims settlement.[4] The ITC also sent a delegation to Alaska to learn from the negotiation process carried out there under the 1971 Alaska Native Claims Settlement Act; the goal was to avoid making any unnecessary mistakes or trade-offs (McComber 2007). In 1976, the ITC submitted a formal proposal to the Government of Canada for the settlement of an Inuit claim that included an item that, at the time, exceeded the bounds of federal land claim policy—the creation of a new territory (Cameron and White 1995; NIC 1995). The ITC determined that land claims negotiations were best facilitated by using regional representative organizations. In 1982, the TFN was created specifically to negotiate the NLCA (INAC 2008). While the ITC (now known as the Inuit Tapiriit Kanatami) represents Inuit interests nationally, the TFN (now under the name Nunavut Tunngavik Incorporated) represents Inuit interests in Nunavut.

The creation of Nunavut represented a key goal for Inuit negotiators of the claim. Inuit communities of the eastern Arctic had long felt alienated from the culturally and geographically distant Government of the Northwest Territories (Henderson 2009; Hicks and White 2015). The federal minister of Indian affairs and northern development made it clear during the negotiations that the Canadian government's support for territorial division was contingent upon popular support for such a motion across the NWT. In 1982, the issue of territorial division was put to a stand-alone, territory-wide plebiscite, the first in NWT history. The plebiscite resulted in a narrow victory (56.48 per cent) for territorial division—with a majority of Indigenous voters in support of Inuit self-determination (Cameron and White 1995, 94). By 1990, an agreement-in-principle on the comprehensive land claims settlement had been reached. The link between the creation of Nunavut and the settlement of the land claim proved to be a point of contention between the

**Table 4.1** Major events in the development of Nunavut

| Year | Event |
| --- | --- |
| 1971 | Inuit Tapirisat of Canada formed |
| 1976 | Inuit land claim declared |
| 1982 | Tunngavik Federation of Nunavut formed; Northwest Territories division plebiscite held |
| 1990 | Agreement-in-principle reached |
| 1992 | Nunavut Political Accord signed |
| 1993 | Nunavut Land Claims Agreement and Nunavut Act signed |
| 1999 | Territory of Nunavut established |

*Source*: Author's own elaboration.

federal government and the TFN. Inuit saw the two demands as inextricably linked, whereas the federal government balked at the idea of the proposed territory being protected by section 35 of the Constitution Act, 1982—which recognizes and affirms treaty rights—as it would give the territory a special constitutional status (Cameron and White 1995). The federal government insisted, given that Nunavut was to be a public rather than an Inuit government, that the new territory and its governance structures would have to be created through a separate act of Parliament. In 1992, a compromise was struck with the signing of the Nunavut Political Accord, which stipulated a deadline of April 1, 1999, for the creation of Nunavut (NIC 1995). In 1993, two pieces of legislation were passed by Parliament to finalize the land claim and create the new territory: the Nunavut Land Claims Agreement and the Nunavut Act.

The NLCA established an Inuit Settlement Area (i.e., the total area of Nunavut) of 1,994,000 km², with direct Inuit ownership (Inuit Owned Land, or IOL) of 356,000 km², or 17.7 per cent of the territory (Bernauer 2019b, 408). Inuit communities have subsurface rights to almost 36,000 km² of IOL, or 1.8 per cent of the territory (Cameron and White 1995, 92).[5] Surface IOLs are managed by regional Inuit associations, while subsurface IOLs are managed by Nunavut Tunngavik Incorporated—the Indigenous corporate organization that represents Inuit interests under the NLCA (Bernauer 2019a, 257). Inuit leaders' willingness to accept a public government model as a form of Indigenous self-government was a condition of the federal government for the creation of Nunavut.[6] Cameron and White (1995, 97) have argued that, "essentially, the Inuit were prepared to accept a modified status quo, with the critical difference that they, not a distant government in Yellowknife, would be in control." According to John Amagoalik, Inuit have a strong dislike of the municipal-type reserve model of self-government found in southern Canada, and they believed that a better financial arrangement with the federal government would be possible under a territorial-type model, with the added advantage that the non-Inuit population was committed to building Nunavut alongside Inuit.[7] A 1992 memo from the TFN revealed the following:

> The Nunavut Agreement does not deliver all that Inuit want or need. However, the Board of Directors of the TFN has carefully weighed the costs and benefits of the Agreement. We are convinced that the Agreement should be approved, because it moves Inuit forward along the path to self-determination. (1992, 2)

In short, Indigenous actors involved in the comprehensive lands claims negotiations viewed Nunavut as a means to achieve self-determination, rather than an end in itself.

## The New Government of Nunavut

Nunavut is home to 39,536 residents, almost 85 per cent of whom are Inuit (Henderson 2009; Timpson 2009b). Iqaluit, the territory's capital, has a population of just 7,740 residents.[8] The population of Nunavut is spread out across twenty-five small communities, many of which are located on islands unconnected by roads. The territory, much of which lies beyond the Arctic Circle, encompasses three time zones and is divided into the same number of administrative regions: Qikiqtani (previously Baffin) in the east; Kivalliq in the centre-west; and Kitikmeot in the far west (White 2009, 290). Yet, Nunavut does not have a regional level of government. By design, there are only two levels—territorial and community—based on the conviction that strong local government must be a fundamental part of the overall structure of government in the territory (NIC 1995, 24). Another notable feature of Nunavut politics is the powerful role played by Nunavut Tunngavik Incorporated (NTI), the successor to the TFN, in the life of the territory. The NTI's prime responsibility lies in the implementation and oversight of the NLCA (Cameron and White 1995). Its leadership is elected on a territory-wide basis, making it accountable to the grassroots.[9] As such, it serves as an unofficial opposition or watchdog organization vis-à-vis the Government of Nunavut. The NTI is the primary legal entity through which Inuit and treaty rights are exercised. It acts as a spokesperson for Inuit. It shares these responsibilities with the territory's three regional associations: Qikiqtani Inuit Association, Kivalliq Inuit Association, and Kitikmeot Inuit Association (Bernauer 2019a).

The creation of the new territory brought with it the task of establishing the Government of Nunavut. As Hicks and White (2015) point out, this was a unique opportunity to fashion a government, practically from the ground up. The Nunavut Implementation Commission (NIC), which was established in 1993, was tasked with overseeing the territorial division planning and the design of the new government (NIC 1995). The NIC was composed of three members nominated by the TFN, three by the Government of Northwest Territories, and three by the federal government, including a chief commissioner acceptable to all parties (Cameron and White 1995). In addition to John Amagoalik, who served as chief commissioner from 1993 to 1999, the NIC counted on the participation of Mary Simon, who, in 2021, became Canada's first Indigenous governor general.[10] The NIC proposed a series of recommendations based on a program of extensive consultations at the leadership and community levels. There was broad consensus on the need for a streamlined, decentralized territorial government, with high priority given to the hiring and training of Inuit residents. According to the NIC (1996, 14), "The Nunavut Government must be designed and implemented so as to be democratically constituted, administratively competent and culturally attuned." As per the NLCA, the new government must also be a public one—meaning a government answerable to a legislative assembly elected by all citizens meeting residence and age qualifications and in which all residents are eligible to vote, hold office, and participate fully in government (NIC 1995; White 1999).

The NIC hoped to address the under-participation of women in territorial politics through its work (Henderson 2009). During the run-up to the establishment of the new government, a gender-parity proposal was put forward to guarantee the equal representation of men and women in the Legislative Assembly. A discussion paper drafted by the NIC noted that in designing a new government, the people of Nunavut had a unique opportunity to find ways of ensuring balanced representation at the highest level; by doing so, the paper pointed out, the Nunavut legislature would be a model for democratic societies everywhere (NIC 1995). The NIC proposed a system based on two-member constituencies in which voters in each electoral district would elect one male and one female member of the Legislative Assembly (MLA). The issue proved contentious. Debates over the proposal included arguments that ranged from the potential of gender parity to restore the traditional balance between women and men in Inuit society to gender equality being a Western concept, foreign to Inuit society (Altamirano-Jiménez 2013). The NIC concluded that any major reforms to established democratic institutions and processes must be based on public support. The proposal was put to a plebiscite in 1997 in which it was rejected by 57 per cent of voters, with a turnout of just 39 per cent (Wilson 2005, 85). In the first three elections following the creation of Nunavut, women made up only 7 per cent of MLAs (White 2013a, 233). Since then, women have made some political gains. Most notably, in 2008, Eva Aariak became Nunavut's first female premier.

The Legislative Assembly of Nunavut, sometimes referred to as "The People's Iglu," resembles other Canadian legislatures, with some notable differences. The Nunavut legislature operates on a non-partisan, consensus basis. Its twenty-two seats are structured in a circle to facilitate consensus-based decision making, as opposed to adversarial rows of benches. According to White (2006, 16), consensus government, which entails a highly participatory process in which decisions emerge through extensive deliberation, bears a family resemblance to deliberative democracy. This legislative design was borrowed from that of the Legislative Assembly of the Northwest Territories, although not automatically (White 2001). In the absence of parties, Nunavut MLAs run as independents in territorial elections. The communities elect the MLAs, and the MLAs then choose the premier and the cabinet—officially known as the Executive Council—in a special session called the Nunavut Leadership Forum (Henderson 2009). The premier assigns the cabinet portfolios. Those MLAs who are not in the cabinet become the de facto opposition.[11] Since 1999, Inuit have been represented in the legislature roughly proportionate to their population size. Inuit MLAs often wear traditional clothing, and much of the business of the legislature is conducted in Inuktitut, with interpretation available to English- and French-language speakers (White 2013b). While the extent to which the legislature operates according to Inuit norms and culture is a matter of debate, the influence of Inuit values and interests on governing practices is a certainty.

Bureaucratic decolonization is a central goal of the new territorial government. Devising a public government that serves Indigenous and non-Indigenous residents alike, however, has proven to be a challenge. The Nunavut government has seen a dramatic increase in the number of Inuit employees within its ranks as a result of targeted employment strategies and progressive language policies. In 2008, the Official Languages Act was adopted by the Legislative Assembly to place Inuktitut on equal footing with English and French. Fluency in this Inuit language has become a de facto requirement for senior public officials at the highest levels of government, though few non-Inuit bureaucrats have more than a rudimentary knowledge of Inuktitut (Timpson 2009a). While the level of Inuit employment within the government now exceeds that of the non-Inuit population (known as *Qallunaat*), much of Inuit employment remains concentrated at the lowest rungs of the public service, in paraprofessional and administrative support positions (White 2009). According to Timpson (2009b, 206), low levels of educational attainment among Inuit, lack of mentoring, and the predominance of English in the workplace are systemic barriers to Inuit employment at representative levels within the new government. Notwithstanding these factors, the government has met its initial target of 50 per cent Inuit employment across all government posts. Nunavut has become the first jurisdiction in Canada to build a public service staffed predominantly by Indigenous people (Timpson 2009b). Tagak Curley has suggested that the public government model has benefited younger generations by encouraging them to become involved in public institutions.[12] For example, in my interview with Shuvinai Mike, director of Inuit Qaujimajatuqangit (IQ) in the Department of Culture and Heritage, she revealed that she had never considered working for the government prior to the establishment of Nunavut.[13]

Inuit traditional knowledge (*Inuit Qaujimajatuqangit*) is the guiding principle of the Government of Nunavut. IQ (as it is commonly referred to in the short-hand) is a transversal policy instrument used to mainstream Inuit rights and cultural values by incorporating them horizontally and systematically at all stages of policy-making and throughout the governance system (Rice 2020). The NIC recommended the creation of departments that would take the lead in translating IQ into public policy. Two departments of particular note were the Department of Sustainable Development (DSD) and the Department of Culture, Language, Elders and Youth (CLEY). Although both departments were central to the creation of Inuit-sensitive institutions of governance, they have since been dismantled. In 2004, the DSD was split to form the Department of the Environment and the Department of Economic Development and Transportation (Timpson 2009a, 202). In 2012, CLEY was restructured into the more conventional Department of Culture and Heritage (Hicks and White 2015, 245). According to Nunavut's Director of IQ, these departmental changes were done without consultation. Interestingly, the Inuktitut signage continues to bear the original names of the departments.[14] In 2001, an IQ Task Force was formed to address the government's failure to treat IQ as a foundational principle in its operations. Its first (and last) annual report called for an IQ senate-type organization to help integrate the Nunavut government into Inuit culture, instead of integrating Inuit into government culture. Members of the task force were not reappointed (Tester and Irniq 2008). The government's restructuring process has essentially left the director of IQ solely responsible for "Inuitizing" government policy and programs.[15] As White (2001, 93) cautions, "how governments do things can be as important as what they do."

Integrating IQ into government policies and programs is a long-term undertaking. Given that there is no precise specification of what this process entails, each department of government has developed its own unique twist to implementing IQ in practice. For instance, the Department of Justice offers community-based policing services, healing circles, and alternative sentencing as a means to incorporate IQ into the legal system. Yet, as Tester and Irniq (2008, 57) point out, the territory's legal system is still a classic adversarial system based on Western legal norms and practices. As part of its commitment to IQ, the Department of Human Resources encourages flexible office hours to allow staff to take time off work to hunt at certain times of the year or to harvest clams when tides are most conducive (White 2006). However, as the director of IQ has pointed out, employees who take advantage of this flexibility do so without pay.[16] According to the report of the IQ Task Force (2002, 1), "The Nunavut public government is fashioned after a model 'borrowed' from the Government of the NWT and other public governments. This is an alien model with its own institutional culture—a culture that impedes the integration of IQ into its service delivery systems." Henderson (2009) has suggested that the extent to which IQ is integrated into the daily workings of the Nunavut government can, in some respects, be seen as a benchmark against which the new territory's efforts to do government differently may be judged.

Perhaps the most unusual design feature of the Government of Nunavut is its high degree of decentralization. A core goal of the creation of the new territory was to bring government closer to the people (Hicks and White 2015; Weber 2014). Decentralization has proven to be an important means of bringing about political and economic development for the territory—and one that is particularly sensitive to the unique political geography of the region. As opposed to administrative decentralization, which is based on the dispersal of policy-making powers, decentralization in Nunavut aimed to geographically disperse government headquarters throughout the territory—in what may more accurately be termed "deconcentration" (Weber 2014). Within three years of the establishment of the Government of Nunavut, over seven hundred well-paid public-sector jobs were either created or transferred to ten small communities outside of the capital city of Iqaluit (Légaré 2008, 361). The relocation of whole units and departments, including mid- and upper-level bureaucratic positions, to remote communities is made possible by Nunavut's state-of-the-art electronic communications systems (White 2001). The result of this "made in Nunavut" solution to the centralization of government operations has been a more even distribution of economic benefits across the population through the provision of training and employment opportunities for local community members. This dynamic has also ensured a more representative level of Inuit employment within the new government by providing Nunavummiut (residents of Nunavut) with the option of remaining in their home communities in a jurisdiction in which the government is the mainstay of the economy (Hicks and White 2015).

## Indigenous Rights and Resource Governance under the Claim

Indigenous rights to autonomy and self-government cannot be fully realized in the absence of land and resource rights. Nunavut has bountiful natural resources, including diamonds, oil, and gas. However, the territory's economic development is stymied by its harsh climate, the vast distances between population centres, and its lack of infrastructure (White 2006). The global climate crisis has wrought increasing environmental changes in the Arctic, enabling the exploitation of remote resource-rich areas that previously were difficult if not impossible to reach. This new access to non-renewable resources, in combination with global energy demands, has increased the pressures that extractive industries exert on Indigenous communities in Nunavut (Ritsema et al. 2015). Since the commodity boom of the early 2000s, natural resource companies have begun to seek out opportunities in regions previously considered too remote or too expensive to operate in profitably, such as northern Canada (Keeling and Sandlos 2015). The extractive industry sector threatens the traditional territories and the livelihoods of Indigenous communities at the same time that it benefits them through economic opportunities. The formal recognition and protection of Indigenous rights, especially with regards to land and natural resources, facilitates meaningful engagement between Indigenous peoples and the state and serves to re-valorize Indigenous political institutions and sovereignty (Pereira and Gough 2013). Comprehensive land claims like the NLCA, which provide legal certainty over land titles and provide avenues for participatory resource governance, are an important mechanism to reconcile a resource-dependent economic model with recognition and respect for Indigenous rights.

Nunavut's co-management and regulatory system is a democratic innovation that promotes Indigenous participation in resource governance. The co-management boards on land, wildlife, and environmental issues were mandated by the NLCA (see table 4.2). The boards are institutions of public government that guarantee extensive Indigenous participation in key policy decisions while maintaining federal control over the use and management of public lands (White 2001, 2008, 2020). The board members are appointed by the NTI and the federal and territorial governments. The jurisdiction of the boards extends to the entirety of Nunavut on such matters ranging from wildlife management to decisions on major economic development projects, including new mines and pipelines (White 2008). While technically the boards are relegated to an advisory role, their decisions are rarely overturned. In a stark example, as White (2001, 92) reports, the 1996 decision of the Nunavut Wildlife Management Board to issue a permit for the legal harvest of a bowhead whale (a species of concern) was put to a test when the federal government came under strong domestic and international pressure to refuse approval of the hunt. Nevertheless, the board's decision stood. Clearly, the claims-mandated boards can, at times, exercise substantial governing authority. Although there is considerable debate over the extent to which the boards incorporate traditional knowledge into their decision-making processes (Nadasdy 2005; Stevenson 2006), the co-management system represents a signal improvement for Inuit in terms of their formal inclusion in governance processes and in providing them with a say on policies that are central to their interests and well-being (White 2020).

The NTI, along with the Governments of Canada and Nunavut, view extractive industry as an important driver of economic growth in the territory. However, as Ritsema et al. (2015) point out, they do so from different vantage points. Whereas the federal government views resource development in the

**Table 4.2** Nunavut land claim boards

| Board name | Seats |
| --- | --- |
| Impact Review Board | 9 |
| Planning Commission | 5 |
| Surface Rights Tribunal | 5 |
| Water Board | 9 |
| Wildlife Management Board | 9 |

*Source*: White (2020, 41).

Arctic as a means to bolster the national economy, the NTI and the territorial government see it as a way to enhance Nunavut's political and economic development. The NLCA enables Inuit communities and their organizations to capture an important share of the wealth produced by the extractive industry sector through the land ownership system and mining and royalty regimes it created. On IOLs with subsurface mineral rights, the beneficiaries of the claim receive all of the royalties from any resource developments. On public lands, which constitute the vast majority of the territory, the federal government collects the resource royalties from extractive activities. In this case, the NLCA provides Inuit organizations with a share of these royalties—50 per cent of the first $2 million received by the federal government and 5 per cent of any further royalties (Bernauer 2019b, 408; NTI 2009). Under the NLCA, resource companies are required to negotiate an Inuit Impact and Benefit Agreement (IIBA) before any project proceeds on IOLs. IIBAs typically include measures to ensure financial compensation and preferential hiring of Indigenous employees and procurement businesses. The IIBAs for surface IOLs are negotiated with the regional Inuit associations, whereas those for subsurface IOLs are negotiated with the NTI (Bernauer 2019a). During the land claims negotiation process, Inuit communities were able to select the surface IOL parcels associated with their specific communities, while the TFN (now the NTI) selected the subsurface IOL parcels, with the assistance of geologists. As a result, subsurface IOLs consist of lands with high mineral and energy resource potential located throughout the territory, with a roughly equal share between each of the three administrative regions (NTI 2009).

The Nunavut government is working to gain jurisdiction over public lands, which would provide it with a significant share of the financial benefit from extractive activities, by seeking a devolution agreement with the federal government (Bernauer 2019b; White 2020). Devolution of authority over lands and natural resources is an essential step in the political and economic development of the territory, and it would provide the territorial government with province-like powers. Devolution agreements took effect in the Yukon in 2003 and the NWT in 2014. The Lands and Resources Devolution Negotiation Protocol, which was signed in 2008 by the Government of Canada, the Government of Nunavut, and the NTI, was the first major step toward devolution in Nunavut. On August 15, 2019, the three parties signed an agreement-in-principle that will serve as the basis for the negotiation of a final devolution agreement.[17] John Amagoalik has indicated that this is part of a larger, four-step plan to be carried out by Inuit leadership: (1) create Nunavut; (2) make the government work; (3) attain devolution; (4) acquire provincial status. While there is no specific timeline for achieving these goals, Amagoalik suggests that Nunavut is still at the second step.[18]

Making Nunavut work entails making life better for Inuit. Daunting social and economic challenges continue to plague the territory. Compared to the rest of Canada, Nunavut has the highest number of people per household; the highest cost of living; the highest crime rate; the highest infant mortality rate; the highest incarceration rate; and the highest suicide rate—close to six times the national average (Department of Justice Canada 2002, 8). Addressing the territory's manifold socio-economic problems is thus the true test of the Nunavut government. According to Cameron and White (1995, 109), Inuit insist that their commitment to Nunavut as an expression of self-determination does not negate the possibility of seeking an Inuit-specific self-government arrangement in the event that the public government system is deemed to have failed.

## Conclusion

Nunavut is a government unlike any other in the Americas. It is a territorial model of government, founded on British parliamentary structures and traditions, that has been modified to meet the values and interests of Inuit in the eastern Arctic. This chapter has sought to explain why Inuit adopted a public government model of Indigenous self-government over an Indigenous form of government, and to understand whether or not the new government is falling short of community expectations. I have suggested that the comprehensive land claims negotiations were coupled with the call for a new territory as a means to secure Inuit economic and political self-determination. In other words, the example of Nunavut teaches us that political autonomy is not possible without economic autonomy. It is important to remember that Inuit, prior to the establishment of the Canadian state, were self-governing and self-sufficient (NIC 1995). Nunavut represents one of the boldest initiatives to restore land and self-government to an Indigenous people. It does so not through an Inuit-specific government but through a partnership between Inuit and non-Inuit society. The territory's establishment has enabled Inuit to achieve far more through the land claims process than any other Indigenous group in Canada (Cameron and White 1995). Notwithstanding these positive developments, Nunavut remains a work-in-progress.

This chapter offers important lessons in the successes and limits of advancing Indigenous rights and representation within the context of state institutions. Nunavut demonstrates the potential for accomplishing Indigenous agendas by way of democratic mechanisms. Inuit have successfully achieved their collective goal of establishing an Inuit homeland through negotiation and compromise, rather than political confrontation and conflict, with the federal and territorial governments. Yet, Nunavut also serves as a sobering reminder of the difficulty of devising a public government that truly meets the needs and expectations of Indigenous peoples, even under relatively favourable conditions (Hicks and White 2015). There is an apparent tension in the Nunavut government between Indigenous ways of knowing and doing and Euro-Canadian governing structures and processes. This has led to a growing concern among Inuit leaders that, in drawing close to the Canadian government, Inuit culture itself will change, especially over subsequent generations, and not the culture of the government.[19] Rethinking the administration of government so as to take Indigenous perspectives seriously will involve building a culture of public government that reflects Indigenous values (Timpson 2009b). A key lesson learned from this experience is that representative democracy is far more flexible and adaptable than is conventionally assumed. As White (2001, 98) points out, democracy's strength lies in its compatibility with a wide range of institutional arrangements rooted in diverse cultures and societies.

# Ecuador: Promoting Plurinationality through Local Indigenous Governments

> *The Ecuadorian state is like a hacienda with a landlord.*
>
> —Delfin Tenesaca, President of ECUARUNARI[1]

The demand for plurinationality that was first made public by Ecuador's Indigenous movement during the 1990 National Indigenous Uprising has succeeded in shining a spotlight on Indigenous rights in the country. Throughout the subsequent decade, Ecuador was widely regarded as the birthplace of Latin America's strongest Indigenous movement (Rice 2012; Van Cott 2005; Yashar 2005). Yet, despite the 2008 constitution's recognition of Ecuador's status as a plurinational state, there has been little progress to date in implementing Indigenous rights to autonomy and self-government, with some scholars even suggesting that a reversal of the gains won in the area of Indigenous rights is now taking place (Martínez Novo 2021). The Ecuadorian state envisions and constrains Indigenous governments, the bedrock of plurinationality, as being essentially in the same position as local or municipal governments. Under this "mini-municipality" model, power is granted to Indigenous governments through a process of delegation and devolved administrative responsibilities rather than in recognition of Indigenous sovereignty (Abele and Prince 2006). In other words, Indigenous communities exercise power under the authority and control of the state. Why did Latin America's strongest Indigenous movement end up with a comparatively weak version of Indigenous autonomy and self-government? And how are Indigenous peoples challenging the limits imposed by the state on Indigenous rights? This chapter takes up these pressing questions.

In tracing these developments, I argue that the lack of political will on the part of Ecuador's central government to implement secondary legislation on Indigenous autonomy and self-government that meets the needs and expectations of the Indigenous movement has produced a system of undefined rights for Indigenous peoples that impedes the construction of a genuinely plurinational state. Under the administration of the left-leaning populist president Rafael Correa (2007–17), state actions to strengthen territorial control as a means to advance the project of "sustainable mining" placed firms limits on Indigenous rights to autonomy (Lalander 2014; Ortiz-T. 2021). Radhuber and Radcliffe (2022, 15) have described this dynamic of centralized state control over resource governance as the "hard kernel of colonial-modern states." As indicated by the words of the former president of the country's main highland Indigenous organization, quoted in this chapter's epigraph, in Ecuador, the president and his allies—largely middle-class intellectuals and technocrats without a background in grassroots politics—tend to run the country in a top-down fashion. In response, the Indigenous movement has looked to local government as a means to generate autonomous spaces. This is perhaps most clearly visible in the repeated electoral victories of the Indigenous-based Pachakutik Movement for Plurinational Unity, now one of Ecuador's longest-standing political parties (Altmann 2016). The control of local space has served to advance a measure of Indigenous autonomy, even if only within the bounds of the legal jurisdiction accorded to municipal governments (Cameron 2009; Van Cott 2008).

The chapter begins by examining the growing calls for plurinationality by Ecuador's Indigenous movement over the course of the 1980s and '90s under the leadership of its national umbrella organization, the Confederation of Indigenous Nationalities of Ecuador (Confederación de Nacionalidades Indígenas del Ecuador, or CONAIE). This section details how Indigenous mobilization, both in the streets and electorally, created a favourable opening for the drafting of a new and innovative constitution in terms of its recognition of the rights of Indigenous peoples and of Nature (Schilling-Vacaflor and Kuppe 2012; Wolff 2012). The chapter then turns to an examination of the slow implementation of those rights in practice as the window of opportunity for change quickly closed after Correa and the Indigenous movement parted ways over their opposing positions on the role of extractive industry in the nation's development plans. Particular attention is paid in this section to the lack of progress made in establishing Indigenous Territorial Circumscriptions—the institutional mechanism outlined in the new constitution for guaranteeing Indigenous rights to autonomy and self-government (Ortiz-T. 2015; Zamora Acosta 2016). The final section of the chapter explores the contested relationship between resource extraction and Indigenous rights to autonomy by examining Correa's controversial Yasuní Ishpingo-Tambococha-Tiputini (Yasuní-ITT) initiative on oil drilling in the Amazon (Caria and Domínguez 2016; Espinosa 2013). The chapter concludes with an overview of the important lessons provided by this case study, especially regarding the need for ongoing social mobilization to close the gap between political discourse and practice on Indigenous rights and representation.

## Protests and Proposals

Ecuador is a country of firsts. It was the first country in Latin America to grant women the right to vote (1929). It was the first country to transition from authoritarianism to democracy (1979) as part of the region's third wave of democratization (Mainwaring 1999). It was also the first country to experience a massive Indigenous uprising (1990) in the contemporary era, and the first to constitutionally recognize (2008) the plurinational character of the state (Rice 2012). It is worth pointing out that Ecuador is one of the smallest countries in South America, both in terms of geographic size (283,560 km$^2$ in total land area) and population (17.64 million in 2020).[2] Yet, Ecuador is a country of incredible cultural and ecological diversity. Estimates of the relative Indigenous population size in Ecuador vary widely depending on the source—ranging from just over 8 per cent of the total population according to the latest government statistics (Merino 2021, 23) to 45 per cent based on CONAIE's estimates (Van Cott 2008, 24)—with most observers suggesting that Indigenous people make up approximately 25 per cent of the country's total population (Deruyttere 1997; Layton and Patrinos 2006).[3] Indigenous peoples in Ecuador are divided along three major ecological zones or regions: coastal, highland, and Amazonian. The Kichwa (sometimes spelled "Quichua") people of the highland region are the country's dominant Indigenous group. The coastal region is home to the Awá, Chachi, and Tsáchila peoples, while the Amazon is the traditional territory of numerous Indigenous nations, including the Shuar, Huaorani, Siona-Secoya, Cofán, and Achuar peoples (Gerlach 2003; Lucero 2008; Selverston 2007). Until relatively recently, Ecuador's Indigenous movement has been able to avoid extensive inter-Indigenous conflict and unite the country's diverse Indigenous communities under the national direction of CONAIE.

CONAIE was formed in 1986 to represent the country's Indigenous peoples at the national level (Collins 2004; Yashar 2005). It did so by unifying the three main regional Indigenous organizations: the Confederation of Indigenous Peoples of the Ecuadorian Amazon, the Coordinator of Indigenous Organizations of the Coast of Ecuador, and the Awakening of the Indigenous Peoples of Ecuador (Ecuador Runacunapac Riccharimui, or ECUARUNARI). CONAIE and the Indigenous movement took centre stage in Ecuadorian politics after the June 1990 National Indigenous Uprising, in which Indigenous groups throughout much of the country participated in weeks-long strikes, marches, and demonstrations as an expression of their frustration with the country's political and economic system (Zamosc 1994). Indigenous identity quickly became the prime reference point for anti-neoliberal contention in the country. Throughout the 1990s—a time of intense structural adjustment for much of Latin America—neoliberal economic policies faltered in Ecuador. Beginning with the government of Rodrigo Borja (1988–92), CONAIE mounted powerful mobilizations against every president who sought to impose market reforms (Mejía Acosta et al. 2008; Silva 2009). Collective action was strengthened in this period by widespread public support for the Indigenous movement. A pattern soon emerged in which the government would announce a policy measure that would prompt mass protests, forcing the government to backtrack on its proposed reforms (Rice 2012). Much like with the first national uprising, the government responded initially with repression and arrests and ultimately with negotiations. According to Indigenous leader Nina Pacari (1996, 24), "This marked the first time in Ecuadorian history that an [I]ndigenous movement forced the government to enter into serious dialogue about national policies."

The idea of forming an Indigenous peoples' political party first developed in the Amazon. In 1995, Amazonian leaders formed their own electoral vehicle to contest elections—the Pachakutik Movement (Van Cott 2005).[4] The decision by Amazonian Indigenous organizations to back Pachakutik in the 1996 general elections forced CONAIE to open up a debate on electoral participation within the Indigenous movement. Electoral reforms in 1994 that eased the restrictions on the formation of new parties prompted Indigenous leaders to reconsider their stance on the issue. After carefully considering the new rules of the game and the demands of its base, CONAIE officially announced the formation of the political arm of Ecuador's Indigenous movement at its 1996 national assembly (Madrid 2012; Rice 2012).

Pachakutik was designed to generate proposals and advance Indigenous and popular-sector interests within the state. Social movement logic, however, permeates and shapes the party's organizational structure and functioning. Pachakutik's candidates all come from social movement backgrounds, ensuring organic ties between the party and its grassroots organizations (Collins 2000). The three main components of Pachakutik's political project are resistance to neoliberalism, anti-corruption, and the creation of a plurinational state (MUPP-NP 2003). Politically, the party pushes for participatory democracy and the decentralization of the state. Economically, it calls for strong state control over the economy and the renegotiation of the foreign debt to allow room for national growth and investment. Socially, the party proposes reforms in education, health care, and working conditions. And juridically, Pachakutik seeks plurinationality, the historic project of the Indigenous movement that would provide Indigenous communities with a measure of autonomy and self-government (MUPP-NP 1999).

In the 1996 general elections—Pachakutik's first electoral outing—the party won an impressive 20.6 per cent of the presidential vote in a campaign that was largely conducted door-to-door. The party also managed to obtain 8 seats in the 82-seat national legislature, making it the fourth-largest bloc (Van Cott 2008). In its strongest electoral performance to date, Pachakutik won the presidential race of 2002 in an electoral coalition with former colonel Lucio Gutiérrez of the Patriotic Society of January 21 party. Gutiérrez had played a leading role in the coup of January 21, 2000, which saw junior military officers join forces with the Indigenous movement to overthrow President Jamil Mahuad (1998–2000) through massive street protests backed by large swatches of civil society (Lucas 2000). However, President Gutiérrez's sudden and unexpected embrace of the neoliberal model once in office saw the governing coalition shattered after Pachakutik stepped down from power just six months after taking office, ultimately undermining the legitimacy and prestige of the nation's once powerful Indigenous movement (Van Cott 2009). In April 2005, Gutiérrez became the third consecutive elected president of Ecuador to be toppled by popular protests in a massive uprising against the direction of his government. In contrast to previous rounds of contention,

**Table 5.1** Indigenous legislators in Ecuador's National Assembly, 1996–2017

| Session | Total number of seats | Number of Indigenous legislators | % of Indigenous legislators |
|---|---|---|---|
| 1996–8 | 82 | 5 | 6.1 |
| 1998–2003 | 120 | 4 | 3.3 |
| 2003–7 | 100 | 9 | 9.0 |
| 2007–9 | 100 | 6 | 6.0 |
| 2009–13 | 137 | 5 | 3.6 |
| 2013–17 | 137 | 9 | 6.6 |

*Source:* Ewig (2020, 5).

however, the Indigenous movement played only a minor role in Gutiérrez's ouster (Becker 2008; Lucero 2008).

In the 2006 general elections, Pachakutik competed on its own and garnered just 2.2 per cent of the presidential vote, highlighting the erosion of the party's national support base (Rice 2012, 57). Instead, the young and charismatic former minister of the economy, Rafael Correa, of the Proud and Sovereign Homeland Alliance, was elected president on a strong anti-neoliberal platform that took up most of the political space formerly occupied by Pachakutik. Correa's so-called Citizens' Revolution—based on the mobilization of the citizenry and the redistribution of political power—eclipsed autonomous organizing efforts in the country (Conaghan 2008). Paradoxically, Correa's assumption of power institutionalized the Indigenous movement's political project while marginalizing the movement itself. There are strong areas of convergence between Correa's and Pachakutik's governing proposals. Both projects are nationalistic and emphasize investment in domestic industries, and both see direct democracy as able to transcend the limits of representative democracy when it comes to advancing popular-sector interests (Jameson 2008). Pachakutik did not field a candidate for the 2009 presidential elections—the first held under the new rules of the 2008 constitution—which saw Correa re-elected by a slim majority. In 2013, Correa was re-elected again with an even stronger majority (Sb and Aravind 2022). Between 2003 and 2017, Pachakutik faced significant challenges to its survival as the party lost its broad social movement support and had to rely more heavily on its Indigenous base (Ewig 2020). Despite these setbacks, Pachakutik continues to serve as an important vehicle for ensuring the consistent presence of Indigenous legislators in Ecuador's National Assembly (see table 5.1).

The gradual disarticulation of Ecuador's Indigenous movement at the national level has resulted in a renewed focus on local governments as a means to generate spaces of autonomy for Indigenous peoples (Ortiz-T. 2021). In a 2012 interview with Rafael Antuni, then the national coordinator of Pachakutik, Antuni suggested that plurinationality continued to be the central theme of the Indigenous movement, with an emphasis on creating or building the plurinational state in practice. In his words, "The state will not erase us."[5] From the beginning, Pachakutik has viewed municipal power as a crucial opportunity for developing governing experience, building up local bases of support, and experimenting with innovative forms of participatory democracy that could potentially be scaled up to higher levels of politics (Cameron 2009). Indeed, the party has garnered international attention for its municipal-level accomplishments. Most notably, the Pachakutik-governed municipality of Cotacachi received the Dubai International Award for Best Practices for democratic innovation and sustainable development in local government in 2000 as well as UNESCO's Cities for Peace Prize for achievements in citizen participation and inclusion in 2002 (Van Cott 2008, 136). Perhaps most impressive, Pachakutik has managed to repeat many of its mayoral victories while expanding its base of support in other regions of the country over time, ensuring its consolidation (Rice 2011b).

## Indigenous Governments and the New Constitution

The passage of the 2008 constitution turned out to be a rare moment of unity between the Indigenous movement and the Correa administration. CONAIE and the Indigenous movement played a pivotal role in developing and defining the concept of the plurinational state in the drafting of the new constitution through the constituent assembly process (Lalander and Lembke 2020). The establishment of a plurinational state was intended to be the cornerstone in a political project of decolonization aimed at replacing the asymmetric relationship between Indigenous peoples and the state with a more horizontal or bilateral one (Acosta 2009; Walsh 2009). Whereas the previous constitution of 1998 had recognized the state as pluricultural and multi-ethnic, the new constitution declared Ecuador a plurinational and intercultural state (Altmann 2016). Interculturality is intended as a bridge-building measure to balance inter-ethnic relationships in a diverse society while also acknowledging the historic and ongoing existence of racism and discrimination.[6] According to Ecuador's renowned Indigenous leader Luis Macas,

> Throughout history, us, the Shuar, Kichwa, and others have had to learn from the dominant culture to survive, including their language. . . . Because of this, we argue that we have to recognize and learn from each other and build from that recognition not homogeneity but interculturality and the normative construction of the plurinational state. . . . The dominant society is only interested in recognizing plurinationality up until a certain point or limit. (2009, 94)

Martínez Novo (2014, 113) has suggested that while the term "plurinational" was accepted by the constituent assembly led by Correa, the constitutional reinforcement of state sovereignty places firm limits on Indigenous autonomy and the representation of Indigenous peoples beyond conventional means of democratic representation.

Ecuador's new constitution institutionalized Indigenous governing practices as part of the state by making an explicit commitment to honouring the Andean Indigenous principle of Living Well (*Buen Vivir* in Spanish; *Sumak Kawsay* in Kichwa), which is based on the values of consensus, respect, and reciprocity between the human and non-human worlds (Fischer and Fasol 2013; Ugalde 2014). According to Lalander (2014), while the principle of Living Well presents an opportunity to bring about an alternative to development, it is being used by the government to justify resource extraction in the name of progressive social welfare programs. Ecuador's development planning document, the National Plan for Living Well (2013–17), envisions sustainable development and the equitable distribution of wealth and resources as the route for attaining the principle of Living Well in practice.[7]

A textual review of the planning document reveals the top three priorities of Correa's administration to be the pursuit of development, human rights, and natural resource wealth. The term "development" is used three times more frequently than the term "Living Well" and is invoked eighteen times more often than the concept of Indigenous autonomy. To advance the long-term goal of Living Well, the government assumes responsibility for the defence of the right to live in a healthy environment and to respect the rights of Nature (Plan Nacional para el Buen Vivir 2013, 16). The National Plan for

Living Well suggests that the principle of Living Well cannot be improvised from below by Indigenous communities, but rather must be planned and managed from above by the state (Plan Nacional para el Buen Vivir 2013, 14). Instead of displacing conventional notions of development based on economic growth, the government has broadened the definition of economic development to include a more balanced relationship between society and the natural world, which it claims can only be brought about by state action (Arsel 2012; Merino 2021).

Prior to Correa's assumption of power, Ecuador had been home to Latin America's most successful example of Indigenous co-management and administration of state funds targeting Indigenous health, education, and development. Ecuador's National Directorate of Intercultural Bilingual Education (Dirección Nacional de Educación Intercultural Bilingüe, or DINEIB) was the first public education institution in Latin America to be headed, staffed, and run by Indigenous people (Chartock 2013). Similarly, the Development Council of the Nationalities and Peoples of Ecuador (Consejo de Desarrollo de las Nacionalidades y Pueblos del Ecuador, or CODENPE) was formed in the 1990s as a semi-autonomous ministry tasked with implementing Indigenous-targeted social funds (Van Cott 2000; Yashar 2005). After taking office in 2007, Correa sought to centralize state authority over the autonomous spaces captured by Indigenous organizations by bringing both DINEIB and CODENPE under presidential control and oversight (Bretón et al. 2022). Following the massive Indigenous-led protests of January 2009 against the government's mining law and its related water reform bill, Correa revoked the legal status of Environmental Action—a leading non-governmental organization—and announced the closure of several Indigenous-run government offices, including CODENPE. DINEIB was then placed under the control of the Ministry of Education (Dosh and Kligerman 2009; Martínez Novo 2014). This move represented a substantial setback for the Indigenous movement as gaining authority over these two offices had been one of its most significant achievements to date (Lucero 2009). From the outset, Correa viewed Indigenous and environmental activism as an obstacle to his program of "progressive extractivism" based on the reinvestment of proceeds from extractive industry in infrastructure and welfare policies and his vision of a socially responsible mining sector as the backbone of the country's development (Lalander, Lembke, and Ospina Peralta 2019).

One of the most frustrating aspects of Indigenous-state relations in contemporary Ecuador remains the lack of progress in instituting the promise of Indigenous Territorial Circumscriptions (Circunscripciones Territoriales Indígenas, or CTIs) contained in both the 1998 and 2008 constitutions. CTIs are special autonomous regimes for the governance of territory based on ethnocultural criteria (Ortiz-T. 2021; Zamora Acosta 2016). They represent an opportunity for Indigenous self-government in Ecuador. The 1998 constitution expressly recognized the collective rights of Indigenous peoples, including the right to form CTIs with the status of political and administrative units of the state. Notwithstanding this commitment, no enabling law to establish and regulate the operational powers of CTIs was ever enacted (Bretón et al. 2022). The 2008 constitution, drafted with the heavy participation of social movements, outlined the procedures for the creation of CTIs and their powers. The petition to constitute a CTI can come from members of an Indigenous people or nation or from a sub-national government (Martínez Novo 2014). The procedure for establishing a CTI is by way of a referendum, with at least two-thirds support from local citizens needed to begin the legal process of transferring governing authority (Ortiz-T. 2015, 61). In 2010, the Organic Code of Territorial Organization, Autonomy, and Decentralization (Código Orgánico de Organización Territorial, Autonomía y Descentralización, or COOTAD), which established a regime of decentralized autonomous governments, added new constraints. The COOTAD limited CTIs to existing territorial units with a majority Indigenous population or the unification of several units to form a new Indigenous majority constituency (Bretón et al. 2022, 18–19). In theory, CTIs can be formed at the parish, municipal, and provincial levels. In practice, however, most analysts agree that the requirements for establishing a CTI are problematic given that only a handful of municipalities in Ecuador have a majority Indigenous population (Zamora Acosta 2016).[8]

Despite legal advances in the procedures and mechanisms for establishing CTIs, to date not a single circumscription has been formed in Ecuador (Ortiz-T. 2021). In the absence of CTIs, the Indigenous movement continues to operate within the existing structures of the state—winning elections and gaining control of local and even regional governments to enact a measure of Indigenous control over their own affairs (Bretón et al. 2022). This dynamic has led some observers to question the utility of CTIs. However, as interviews with Indigenous leaders have made clear, the Indigenous movement desires a form of autonomy based not on parishes and municipalities but on CTIs that respect Indigenous peoples' traditional territories.[9] Such territories are much larger than municipalities; as such, the Indigenous movement's understanding of and expectations for CTIs would require the redrawing of political and administrative units of the state (Radhuber and Radcliffe 2022). This vision of CTIs is more in tune with conceptualizations of self-determination and territorial rights established in international agreements, such as the International Labour Organization's Convention 169 and the United Nations Declaration on the Rights of Indigenous Peoples (Ortiz-T. 2015; Zamora Acosta 2016). The legal framework established by the 2008 constitution, as well as the secondary legislation in force, such as COOTAD, have simplified and narrowed the Indigenous movement's demand for autonomy and self-government to fit within the confines of a liberal system of "low-scale autonomies" (Altmann 2016, 130). According to Abele and Prince (2006, 573), "We have encountered no Aboriginal nations, no matter how small, that have identified the mini-municipality model as their ultimate goal." At best, the limited model of autonomy and self-government in effect in Ecuador may serve as a stepping stone to the realization of full Indigenous self-government with a wide range of governing powers.

## Resource Extraction and Indigenous Peoples

In Ecuador, as throughout much of Latin America, the state retains control over subsurface mineral, oil, and gas resources, including those found within Indigenous territories. De Sousa Santos (2009, 59) has argued that Indigenous autonomies must have control over resources within their territories, "otherwise their autonomy will be empty." Following the 2008 constitution, Indigenous communities have the right to free, prior, and informed consultation—but not consent—concerning planned measures affecting them, such as natural resource extraction (Lalander 2014; Shade 2015). Ecuador's consultation regime is marked by the two-way exchange of information between project proponents and Indigenous community members. Despite the presence of dialogue, however, the option of supporting or rejecting the proposed development is off the table (Szablowski 2010). In other words, consent is sought but not required. In addition to the right to prior consultation (article 57.7), the new constitution enshrined the inalienability of traditional or "intangible" lands (article 57.4). According to article 57,

The territories of the peoples living in voluntary isolation are an irreducible and intangible ancestral possession and all forms of extractive activities shall be forbidden there. The State shall adopt measures to guarantee their lives, enforce respect for self-determination and the will to remain in isolation and to ensure observance of their rights. The violation of these rights shall constitute a crime of ethnocide, which shall be classified as such by the law.

The challenge in Ecuador lies in the unwillingness on the part of the government to ensure that Indigenous peoples' territorial rights are upheld and respected in practice (Sieder 2016). As a student activist noted in my interview with him, there are two issues that the Correa government did not understand: citizen participation and the environment.[10]

The outcome of Correa's Yasuní-ITT initiative reveals the troublesome contradictions between official discourse on Indigenous and environmental rights and the government's development practices and priorities on the ground. In 2007, Correa launched an innovative conservation initiative with global implications. His government proposed to permanently suspend oil extraction in a portion of the Amazonian Yasuní National Park in exchange for monetary compensation on the part of the international community equivalent to half of the estimated USD 7 billion that the Government of Ecuador would have grossed from its development (Caria and Domínguez 2016; Espinosa 2013). The stated aim of the initiative was to conserve the incredibly rich biodiversity of the zone, protect Indigenous communities living in voluntary isolation (namely the Huaorani people), and to avoid the climate costs associated with the massive release of carbon dioxide emissions from oil extraction. Despite partnering with the United Nations Development Program (UNDP) to administer the Yasuní-ITT Fund, the response of the international community was underwhelming. On 15 August 2013, Correa officially abandoned the initiative, citing poor follow through by the world's wealthy nations. On 3 October 2013, the Ecuadorian National Assembly gave its approval to commence oil drilling in the national park (Lalander 2014). The decision to move ahead with oil exploitation in a protected area of the Amazon tarnished Ecuador's reputation as a global environmental and Indigenous rights leader.

Indigenous and environmental activists in Ecuador have continued to oppose the government's resource development plans in Yasuní National Park. CONAIE has argued, to little avail, that the government has systematically disregarded constitutionally protected Indigenous rights in this case. As Sieder (2016) points out, constitutional provisions in the absence of secondary legislation and coherent technical rules, in conjunction with an economic development model premised on the exploitation of natural resources, has meant that proclamations of Indigenous rights have amounted to empty promises. In response, the Quito-based anti-extractivist group Yasunidos launched a national campaign to force a referendum on the issue. However, in May 2014, the National Electoral Council disqualified the group's submission after finding a number of irregularities in the signatures that had been gathered (Merino 2021). The Ecuadorian government then moved to the second phase of active exploration and drilling in the zone, further widening the distance and divisions between the Correa administration and civil society actors in the country (Rice 2019).

On May 24, 2017, Lenín Moreno, former vice-president under Rafael Correa, became president of Ecuador. President Moreno was elected on a platform that aimed to "dignify politics" by promoting a less confrontational approach to governing than that of his predecessor (Borja and Davidsen 2018). Moreno was Latin America's first paraplegic head of state and had previously been nominated for a Nobel Peace Prize for his advocacy on behalf of persons with disabilities. In June 2017, Moreno launched a national dialogue that included a discussion with social movement organizations, journalists, and opposition leaders on pressing national issues (Sb and Aravind 2022). As part of this initiative, Moreno solicited questions and proposals from the public. The issue of oil drilling in Yasuní National Park re-emerged as a prominent public concern. Moreno subsequently proposed putting the protection of the park to a public consultation, along with six other key national questions ranging from term limits for public authorities to barring individuals involved in corruption from running for office to banning mining in protected areas and urban centres (see table 5.2). Moreno encouraged Ecuadorians to vote yes on all the issues. The national referendum and public consultation that was held on February 4, 2018, resulted in a resounding victory for Indigenous and environmental groups. In response to the question on dramatically reducing the amount of oil drilling allowed in the Yasuní-ITT, 67.3 per cent voted in favour, with 32.7 per cent opposed. Regarding the question on prohibiting

**Table 5.2** Ecuadorian referendum and popular consultation results, 2018

| Questions | Yes (%) | No (%) |
|---|---|---|
| **Referendum on reforms to the 2008 constitution** | | |
| 1. Do you agree with a lifetime ban for people convicted of corruption from serving in public office? | 73.7 | 26.3 |
| 2. Do you agree with the elimination of the possibility of unlimited re-election? | 64.2 | 35.8 |
| 3. Do you agree with the restructuring and renewal of the Council of Citizen Participation and Social Control? | 63.1 | 36.9 |
| 4. Do you agree to the removal of the statute of limitations for sexual crimes against children and adolescents? | 73.5 | 26.5 |
| 5. Do you agree to the prohibition of metallic mining in all its stages in protected areas, intangible zones, and urban centres? | 68.6 | 31.4 |
| **Popular consultation on issues of national importance** | | |
| 6. Do you agree with the elimination of the tax over capital gains on real estate property? | 63.1 | 36.9 |
| 7. Do you agree to increase the intangible zone by at least 50,000 hectares and reduce the area of oil exploration authorized by the National Assembly in the Yasuní National Park from 1,030 hectares to 300 hectares? | 67.3 | 32.7 |

*Source*: Jaramillo (2018, 3).

metallic mining in protected areas, intangible zones, and urban centres, 68.6 per cent were in support and 31.4 per cent were against. While innovative in its approach to consultation on Indigenous rights issues, the dilution of Indigenous decision-making authority into the larger body politic through the mechanism of a national referendum is nonetheless problematic.

In 2019, Moreno's presidential approval rating plummeted amid a growing economic crisis resulting from the collapse of commodity prices. Moreno moved to renegotiate agreements with the International Monetary Fund and instituted austerity measures that triggered a wave of discontent (Lalander, Lembke, and Ospina Peralta 2019; Sb and Aravind 2022). In October 2019, following an attempt by the government to remove oil and gas subsidies, a massive popular uprising led by CONAIE forced Moreno to leave the capital city of Quito and temporarily move his office to the coastal city of Guayaquil, restoring to the Indigenous movement much of its lost power (Bretón et al. 2022). Moreno, whose popularity dipped into the single digits following the ravages of the COVID-19 pandemic in the country, chose not to seek re-election in 2021. Instead, former director of Ecuador's Central Bank and minister of knowledge and human talent under Correa, Andrés Arauz, entered the race with the backing of the former president. Arauz's main competitor on the political left was Indigenous environmental activist Yaku Pérez of Pachakutik. Pérez—a former president of ECUARUNARI who was elected prefect of Azuay Province in 2019—became a popular political figure during Correa's presidency by protesting controversial mining projects, particularly in his hometown of Cuenca, in the southern highlands. Pérez and Pachakutik narrowly missed securing a spot in the presidential runoff between the top two contenders (Rice 2021). Arauz ultimately lost that election to the social conservative and pro-business candidate Guillermo Lasso. Lasso, who assumed the presidency on May 24, 2021, became the country's first centre-right president in nearly two decades. Pachakutik, which has once again taken up its spot as the country's main opposition party, is now the second-largest bloc in the National Assembly.

## Conclusion

In terms of Indigenous rights, Ecuador was once the bright spot in South America—the country with the most advanced protections, policies, and programs for Indigenous peoples in the region (a position now occupied by Bolivia). This chapter has sought to explain why Ecuador's constitutional promises of Indigenous autonomy and self-government remain unfulfilled. I have suggested that governing elites in Ecuador have actively worked to stymie the implementation of Indigenous rights legislation, particularly in the area of territorial autonomy and resource rights. The recognition of the plurinational state is certainly an important step toward improving Indigenous-state relations in the country, but the problems of slow implementation and lack of political will have produced a contentious and unfinished process of state transformation (Martínez Novo 2021; Merino 2021). Plurinationality was envisioned by CONAIE and the Indigenous movement as the transverse axis of the organizational structure of the state, influencing forms of participation, representation, inclusion, and decision making (Acosta 2009; Resina de la Fuente 2012). Instead, as Indigenous leader Delfin Tenesaca has noted, the Ecuadorian state continues to operate in a pyramidal form, with Indigenous communities at the bottom of the hierarchy.[11] State limitations on the practice of Indigenous autonomy have essentially relegated Indigenous governments to the realm of municipal politics (Martínez Novo 2014).

The roller coaster of Indigenous politics in Ecuador teaches us a number of valuable lessons about pushing the boundaries of state limits on Indigenous rights. First, this case study highlights the importance of electoral and protest coalitions in creating favourable windows of opportunity for institutional change. Ecuador's Indigenous movement has participated in party politics—winning elections at all levels of government—in addition to leading massive protest campaigns resulting in policy negotiations and the broadening of political agendas to include Indigenous rights issues (Merino 2021; Rice 2012). Second, the case offers us a sobering reminder of the importance of the willingness of the party in power to implement changes. The governing agenda of President Correa, for example, was plagued by contradictions and ambiguities. While his administration expanded Indigenous rights, at least in theory, the process for obtaining them in practice proved frustrating, and at times ultimately fruitless (Martínez Novo 2014; Ortiz-T. 2015). Lastly, the study of Indigenous politics in Ecuador reveals the need for ongoing social mobilization to close the gap between political discourse and practice. In the instructive example of Ecuador's Yasuní National Park, the Indigenous movement succeeded in protecting the park from expanded oil operations by mobilizing around the contradictions between official discourse on the rights of Nature and the principle of Living Well, on the one hand, and the resource-dependent, state-led model of development pursued by the government, on the other (Lalander 2014; Rice 2019). While for the moment the fight for Indigenous autonomy and self-government appears to have reached an impasse in Ecuador, the return of Pachakutik at the ballot box and of CONAIE in the streets of the capital city indicate that the country will continue to be a beacon of Indigenous and democratic governance innovation for the foreseeable future.

# CONCLUSION

## Instituting Indigenous and Democratic Governance Innovations

Settler colonialism is a structure—an organizing principle—that has been harmful to Indigenous communities throughout the Americas. This book set out to understand how to decolonize our democracies based on the insights and experiences of powerful and inspiring Indigenous movements in Bolivia, Ecuador, Nunavut, and Yukon—arguably the most successful cases of the institutional pathway to Indigenous autonomy and self-government in the Americas. In so doing, I have taken up the call of Abele and Prince (2006, 572) "to encourage others to give consideration to this issue and to these models." The four models of Indigenous autonomy and self-government highlighted in this book have proven to be important clarifying devices allowing us to compare approaches to self-determination across wide variations in levels of social and economic development, welfare states, democratic traditions, political cultures, and histories. As I conclude this study, however, there remain two pressing questions: What are the factors that produce distinctive pathways to Indigenous autonomy and self-government, and ultimately, to democratic decolonization? And what are the possibilities for change beyond the state? Based on the case study evidence presented in previous chapters, I might venture a few tentative answers.

The findings of this study speak to some of the thorniest issues in democratic governance. Among the most pressing problems facing contemporary democracies is the accommodation of Indigenous peoples' rights, interests, and aspirations (White 2020). Indigenous movements are pushing the democratic envelope in a way that ensures greater inclusion and participation for some of society's most marginalized groups. A central objective of the book has been to assess whether Indigenous-state relations are improving in the cases under consideration on the basis of mutual recognition and respect.

For the most part, I have found that they have improved in the cases of Bolivia, Nunavut, and Yukon, and to a lesser extent in the case of Ecuador, though the results remain partial and uneven. The study also revealed the myriad ways that states have attempted to address demands for democratic decolonization by constraining them to fit within the confines of liberal institutions. These findings highlight a key paradox of the process of democratic decolonization—the tension between the desire to uproot colonialism and its legacies and the use of liberal state mechanisms to do so (Eversole 2010; Postero 2017). The examples of Indigenous and democratic governance innovation explored in the book, ranging from wildlife co-management boards to Indigenous-run state institutions, indicate that it is possible for Indigenous peoples to realize an important measure of self-determination within the institutional contexts and state structures in which they live. However, these hard-won spaces of autonomy are subject to reversals and rollbacks by the state unless closely monitored and constantly challenged by Indigenous movements and organizations.

This concluding chapter begins with an analysis of the factors that led to the different pathways to Indigenous autonomy and self-government in the book's comparative case studies. Case-specific combinations of structural, institutional, and agency-oriented factors are suggested to have shaped the particular model of Indigenous autonomy in each instance. The next section of the chapter addresses the democratic implications of Indigenous demands for autonomy and self-government. This section also revisits the question posed in the book's introduction on how the project of decolonization unsettles the practice of democracy. Based on case study findings, I argue that the promotion of Indigenous rights and representation does not undermine democracy or the state—it may in fact strengthen them. The final section of the chapter looks at potential alternative pathways to bring about change, as well as future research agendas in comparative and Indigenous political inquiry.

## Institutional Pathways to Indigenous Autonomy and Self-Government

The four models of Indigenous autonomy and self-government featured in this book embody different power relations between Indigenous peoples and the state. Yukon's nation-to-nation approach to self-government is based on bilateral relations between individual First Nations and the federal government in which the powers of Indigenous self-determination are generally recognized as deriving outside of and prior to the Canadian state (Abele and Prince 2006, 580). In many respects, this model represents the ideal institutional arrangement. In contrast, Bolivia's third-order approach and Nunavut's public government model are based on differing degrees of Indigenous self-governing power within the state. In both cases, Indigenous peoples exercise a strong measure of control over their own affairs, but only up until a certain point or state-imposed limit. Lastly, Ecuador's local or municipal-style approach to autonomy and self-government is predicated on powers of self-determination that are under the authority and control of the state. According to Abele and Prince (2006, 585), the mini-municipality model represents the least desirable form of Indigenous autonomy and self-government. Given that each of these models contains different possibilities for and constraints on self-determination, how did Bolivia, Ecuador, Nunavut, and Yukon end up with their particular model of Indigenous autonomy and self-government? I propose that the outcomes of Indigenous struggles for autonomy and self-government examined in this study can in large part be explained by three main factors: (a) the choices and preferences of the actors themselves; (b) the willingness of the state to share power with Indigenous peoples; and (c) the availability of power-sharing institutions.

In Nunavut and Yukon, the state was highly motivated to negotiate with Inuit and First Nations over outstanding land claims. In contrast to most Canadian provinces in the South, Indigenous peoples throughout much of the North did not sign historical treaties with the Crown, nor did they receive reserve lands (Cameron and White 1995; White 2020). As a result, Indigenous peoples in these regions are eligible to negotiate comprehensive land claims— modern-day treaties—with greater potential for significant powers of self-determination. Alcantara (2013, 81) has suggested that the federal government, which in the late 1970s became interested in settling northern land claims as a means to develop the region's natural resources, was under the impression that Yukon First Nations were likely to complete an agreement quickly and in accordance with the preferences of the Canadian government. Instead, as chapter 2 revealed, Yukon First Nations became involved in a protracted negotiation process that broke down at one point over the federal government's proposed third-order model of self-government. Yukon First Nations, who have a history of distinct identities and a desire for self-government that reflect these distinctions, held out until they achieved the greatest possible degree of Indigenous autonomy and self-government under a nation-to-nation model.

In contrast, in Nunavut, Indigenous peoples expressed a clear preference for exercising their powers of self-determination within the state in exchange for the creation of a new territory. As chapter 4 outlined, Nunavut's public government model works to advance Indigenous autonomy and self-government as the demographic superiority of the Inuit population ensures effective Indigenous control over the territorial government.

In Bolivia and Ecuador, where there is no history of treaty relations between Indigenous peoples and the state, Indigenous peoples pursued plurinationality through constitutional reform. The essence of plurinationality is the sharing of power (Resina de la Fuente 2012, 154). By choosing the electoral path to change, Indigenous movements in both countries opted to work within the institutions of the state. As detailed in chapter 3, Bolivia's Indigenous-backed Movement toward Socialism managed to project itself onto the national political stage during a period of intense social mobilization in the early 2000s. Under the leadership of the country's first Indigenous president, Evo Morales, Indigenous peoples attained the maximum degree of power within the state through a third-order model of Indigenous autonomy and self-government. In contrast, in Ecuador, social mobilization against neoliberalism led to the election of the populist and left-leaning presidency of Rafael Correa, a non-Indigenous politician. Correa's technocratic approach to policy-making, detailed in chapter 5, resulted in the implementation of some of the Indigenous movement's central demands while undermining the role of Indigenous peoples in Ecuadorian politics and society. Despite a constitutional commitment to Indigenous self-government, not one Indigenous Territorial Circumscription has yet been established. Instead, the Indigenous movement has sought a measure of autonomy through locally elected governments. Clearly, Ecuador's model of Indigenous autonomy and self-government does not meet the preferences and expectations of the country's once-powerful Indigenous movement. However, the recent resurgence of widespread Indigenous mobilization and the return of the Indigenous-based Pachakutik party as a viable electoral option indicates that a more transformational model of Indigenous autonomy and self-government may one day be possible.

## Indigenous Politics and Democratic Decolonization

What are the democratic implications of Indigenous demands for autonomy and self-government? The rise of Indigenous peoples as important new social and political actors is a positive trend in contemporary democracies. Rather than seeking to overthrow the state, Indigenous activists and movements are looking to transform state power and, in so doing, reform democracy to make it fit their hopes and dreams (Cairns 2000; Yashar 1999). A major theme that has arisen out of this study is the vibrancy of Indigenous politics, in relation to and beyond the state. Indigenous leaders in Bolivia, Ecuador, Nunavut, and Yukon play a dual political role in their respective societies—nurturing their internal capacities of self-governance while engaging with the institutional processes of settler states. This difficult balancing act is an essential ingredient for democratic decolonization. The outcome of the unique approaches to Indigenous autonomy and self-government being taken in northern Canada and the central Andes is the blending of classical features of liberal democracy with new institutional arrangements arising from the distinct societies and cultures in these regions (Cameron and White 1995). Liberal or representative democracy is far more flexible and adaptable than is normally assumed. The findings presented in this book challenge the notion that there is a single liberal end point to democratic development or one superior model of democracy—rather, as these case studies have shown, there are many variations and pathways to greater democratization (O'Donnell 2010).

The experiences of democratic decolonization explored in this book suggest that one of the ways that decolonization unsettles the practice of democracy is by placing new demands on the political system. The inclusion of Indigenous peoples in the structures of the state has opened up the policy-making process to citizen participation, deliberation, and decision making, and promoted the growth of new forms of society-centred governance (Merino 2021; White 2020). Indigenous self-government arrangements of the varieties examined here have resulted in more complex forms of governance in Canada and Latin America that have ultimately made democracy more meaningful for its citizens. Indigenous movements in these regions have also pressured states to recognize and institutionalize a more differentiated citizenship regime, one that can accommodate both individual and collective rights (Oxhorn 2011; Yashar 2005). As such, Indigenous politics is effecting a fundamental rethinking of the homogenizing and liberal underpinnings of citizenship regimes and the state as part of its "postliberal challenge" (Yashar 2005). According to Yashar (2005, 285–6), "Viewed as a whole, the postliberal challenge compels us to consider the coexistence of multiple national identities associated with national citizenship, multiple modes of interest intermediations, and multiple institutional sites formally vested with political power and jurisdiction." In short, Indigenous politics has breathed diversity into our democratic ideas, practices, and processes, expanding our political imagination beyond the state (Picq 2017).

The final theme that has emerged out of this book is how participation in institutionalized politics affects Indigenous activism, as well as how activists change democratic institutions. As the case studies in this book have demonstrated, protest broadens and expands democracy by including new actors, issues, and agendas in the political system. The combination of electoral participation and protest politics that is the hallmark of Indigenous political dynamics in Bolivia and Ecuador, and to a lesser extent in Nunavut and Yukon, has served to create important windows of opportunity for institutional change in these cases. Indigenous activists have capitalized on these political openings by introducing key governance innovations into their respective political systems, including, for example, the recognition of the rights of Nature, reserved seats for Indigenous people, official use of Indigenous languages, and the introduction of legal pluralism. As Montúfar (2006) reminds us, while agents of representative democracy tend to prefer the status quo, civil society actors are more likely to propose and act on new initiatives. By channelling Indigenous demands into the political system, governments in northern Canada and the central Andes have enhanced their democratic performance and legitimacy.

## Possibilities for Change beyond the State

The case studies presented in this book do not represent the only possibility or pathway to effect change in contemporary democracies. Alternatives to institutional participation abound in the Americas. A central dilemma faced by Indigenous movements is whether to retain an oppositional stance to their respective political systems or to try to bring about change by way of the democratic mechanisms already in place (Rice 2012; Yashar 2005). An institutional strategy is conventionally assumed to risk the loss of movement legitimacy and autonomy as Indigenous groups submit themselves to the rules and regulations of the largely alien political system that has long served as an instrument of domination and oppression (Ladner 2003; Massal and Bonilla 2000). In the words of Indigenous scholar and activist Leanne Betasamosake Simpson (2017, 50), "I am not interested in inclusion. I am not interested in reconciling. I'm interested in unapologetic place-based nationhoods using Indigenous practices and operating in an ethical and principled way from an intact land base." Likewise, Taiaiake Alfred (2005) has suggested that statist solutions, such as self-government and land claims agreements, are aspects of a "politics of pity." According to Alfred (2005, 20), "Conventional and acceptable approaches to making change are leading us nowhere."

In Canada, distinct relationships between Indigenous peoples and the state have shaped differing stances on the merits and limits of engaging with the institutions of the settler state. While First Nations tend to seek nation-to-nation political relations with the state, others, such as Inuit and Métis, have historically been more willing to participate in Canadian political institutions (Cairns 2000; Papillon 2008). The political behaviour of Indigenous groups also varies tremendously across provinces and territories. For instance, in northern Canada, where Indigenous candidates compete in elections, turnout rates of Indigenous voters often exceed those of non-Indigenous residents; whereas in southern Canada, the stronger discourse on Indigenous nationalism that permeates Indigenous communities results in lower levels of electoral participation (Guérin 2003; Ladner 2003). Indigenous scholar Glen Coulthard (2014) has argued that the relationship between Indigenous peoples and the Canadian state remains colonial to its core despite the presence of a wide range of recognition-based mechanisms to address concerns related to Indigenous rights within the political system.

In Latin America, Indigenous peoples have turned their backs on electoral politics as a means of advancing the Indigenous agenda most notably in Mexico and Guatemala. In Mexico, the Indigenous-based Zapatista Army of National Liberation distanced itself from the state and mainstream political parties following the breakdown of negotiations in the mid-1990s over issues of autonomy and self-government within Indigenous communities. The Zapatistas have instead turned inward in an attempt to build de facto autonomous communities, largely isolating the Indigenous cause from the national political agenda (Gómez Tagle 2005; Nash 2001). In Guatemala, Indigenous communities voted down a proposed constitutional amendment that included the recognition of Indigenous rights in the referendum of 1999. Although there was considerable variation among rural and urban voters, Warren (2002) has suggested that the no vote on the part of Maya communities reflected their skepticism of the electoral process as an effective means of bringing about change. Instead, Mayas are working to find alternative avenues of political influence by building a grassroots movement based on cultural revitalization. While alternative approaches or pathways to Indigenous autonomy and self-government are beyond the scope of this study, they are important to take into consideration when doing democracy differently.

## Looking Ahead

The findings of this study offer important takeaways for political science. Echoing Falleti (2021), our discipline needs to devote more attention and resources to the study of Indigenous politics or risk missing the transformations that Indigenous peoples are bringing about, from the local level to the international arena. The study of institutions has long been a mainstay of political science research. Yet, the concern with formal institutions and the measurement of attitudes regarding these institutions are insufficient to understand the contributions that Indigenous peoples are making to the study of politics and power (Deloria and Wilkins 1999). As Cameron (2018) has so aptly pointed out, our political institutions are failing to respond to some of the biggest challenges of our times. Keme (2018) has suggested that the colonial logic that erases Indigenous peoples persists as a central organizing principle of states and their hegemonic institutions. A new research agenda on political institutions is desperately needed—one that can address certain crucial questions: Whose interests do our political institutions serve? Whose rights do they protect and enforce? And how can their failings be addressed so that they come to serve different purposes? By paying greater attention to such areas of study as Indigenous law, nationalism, sovereignty, and land-based politics, we would greatly expand the conceptual resources available to the discipline of political science (Ferguson 2006).

A critical insight of this study is the importance of Indigenous ownership and control over surface and subsurface natural resources for experiments in Indigenous autonomy and self-government to flourish. The strong overlap between mineral deposit locations and Indigenous communities in Canada and Latin America ensures that the intersection of Indigenous rights and extractive industry will be a critical avenue of comparative research in the years to come (Rice 2019; Szablowski 2010). There are also interesting parallels between Indigenous-corporate partnerships in the resource sector in Canada's northern territories and Latin America's model of progressive extractivism that warrant greater analytical attention (Bernauer 2019b; Keely and Sandlos 2015). More research is needed on the convergence of Indigenous and environmental activism in response to extractive activities (Clapperton and Piper 2019; Eisenstadt and Jones West 2019), as well as the increasing criminalization of these protest actions (Arce and Nieto-Matiz 2024; Lindt 2023). The transnational dimension of Indigenous movement struggles is also a neglected area of research (Silva 2013), as are the political consequences of social protest (Bosi, Giugni, and Uba 2016). A new research agenda that addresses whether or not Indigenous protests against extractive industry operations lead to policy changes, for instance, would do much to advance the literature on Indigenous politics. The results of this research agenda would have relevance to ongoing scholarly debates as well as practical implications for policy-making.

Doing democracy differently also means doing better by Indigenous women. More comparative research is needed on Indigenous self-determination, governance, and gender, including the tensions between collective and individual rights to autonomy (Kuokkanen 2019). We still know comparatively little about the internal dynamics of Indigenous movements and organizations. Recent work on Indigenous women's movements is beginning to pry open the black box of Indigenous mobilization to reveal important gendered dynamics (Hernández Castillo and Speed 2006; Rousseau and Morales Hudon 2017). Research in this area has also begun to address the pressing issue of the causes and consequences of violence against Indigenous women in Canada and Latin America (García Del Moral 2018; Sieder 2011). Despite recent legal and constitutional gains, Indigenous women continue to face gendered violence from public and private actors, as well as from their own domestic partners (Speed 2016). Indigenous women are often at the forefront of violent confrontations with state and private security forces seeking to evict them from their lands to make way for economic development projects (Arteaga Böhrt 2023; Figueroa Romero and Hernández Pérez 2023; Fregoso and Bejarano 2009). Violence against Indigenous women is a multi-faceted problem, requiring a multi-faceted solution. More research is needed on how to design effective strategies for the prevention and elimination of gendered and colonial violence, including alternative solutions based on cultural models of dialogue and reparations as a means to guarantee access to justice (Guimont Marceau et al. 2020). Future research must tell these stories.

## Conclusion

On a practical level, all states in the Americas are grappling with the issue of Indigenous autonomy and self-government. Accordingly, this book speaks to some of the practical aspects of implementing Indigenous self-governance in

Canada and Latin America, as well as some of the theoretical and normative questions about democratic possibilities and the kind of society in which we wish to live (Cameron 2018). The emergence of powerful Indigenous rights movements should be viewed as an opportunity to deepen the regions' democracies. Indigenous political engagement is challenging exclusionary state structures and highlighting the failure to incorporate, represent, and respond to important segments of the population. Indigenous movements in the cases examined in this book have sought to transform the nature of state power. In Canada, the experiments in diversifying democracy that are taking place in the northern territories have the potential to spark innovation in the southern provinces and beyond. In Latin America, the demand for plurinationality that originated in the central Andes and that is now spreading to neighbouring countries may be a means to improve democratic participation and inclusion in the region. This will surely benefit Indigenous communities as well as serve the interests of the broader society.

The major appeal of the structured, focused comparative approach employed in this study—based on a variation of the "most different systems" research design involving the study of similarities across structurally different cases—is that it is capable of producing broad generalizations on Indigenous politics (Collier and Mahoney 1996). The case studies analyzed in the book reveal a number of lessons that may be relevant to Indigenous movements and organizations elsewhere. First and foremost, participation in party politics and the pursuit of Indigenous autonomy and self-government are not mutually exclusive endeavours. The positive institutional outcomes of Indigenous rights struggles in Bolivia, Ecuador, Nunavut, and Yukon demonstrate the potential for accomplishing Indigenous agendas by way of democratic mechanisms. Second, building nation-to-nation relationships between Indigenous peoples and settler states requires constructing institutions that are both culturally appropriate and shared. Improving Indigenous-state relations demands a willingness to work together and to share obligations and responsibilities on the part of Indigenous and settler governments. Lastly, ongoing Indigenous mobilization is needed to close the gap between official discourse and practice on Indigenous rights and representation that exists in contemporary democracies. My hope for this book is that it generates bold new questions and approaches in the study of comparative and Indigenous politics that will serve the needs of academics and activists alike.

# Notes

NOTES TO INTRODUCTION

1   Author interview, Whitehorse, Yukon, June 8, 2012.

2   Author interview, Iqaluit, Nunavut, June 6, 2013.

3   Author interview, La Paz, Bolivia, August 22, 2014.

4   Author interview, Quito, Ecuador, August 27, 2012.

5   Notable exceptions include important comparative studies of Indigenous politics in Canada and Mexico. See especially Altamirano-Jiménez (2013) and Cook and Lindau (2000).

6   The Bolivia's 2009 constitution can be consulted online at https://pdba.georgetown.edu/Constitutions/Bolivia/bolivia09.html.

7   The 2008 Ecuadorian Constitution is available at http://pdba.georgetown.edu/Constitutions/Ecuador/english08.html.

NOTES TO CHAPTER 1

1   Abele and Prince (2006) do not identify self-governing First Nations in the Yukon as embodying the nation-to-nation model. Instead, the authors outline the key features of this model and the power relations that it embodies.

2   Author interview, La Paz, Bolivia, August 22, 2014.

NOTES TO CHAPTER 2

1   Author interview, Whitehorse, Yukon, June 5, 2012.

2   Dietmar Tramm, senior policy analyst, Kwanlin Dün First Nation Government, author interview, Whitehorse, Yukon, June 18, 2012.

3   See "Census 2021," Yukon Bureau of Statistics, accessed January 20, 2024, https://yukon.ca/en/statistics-and-data/yukon-bureau-statistics/find-yukon-statistics-statcan-census.

4   It was exactly a hundred years later, in 2002, that the Ta'an Kwäch'än First Nation signed its final land claim and self-government agreements. See "A Short History of the Ta'an Kwäch'än," Ta'an Kwäch'än Council, accessed January 21, 2024, https://taan.ca/history/.

5   Author interview, Whitehorse, Yukon, June 20, 2012.

6   See "History of Land Claims," Council of Yukon First Nations, accessed January 21, 2024, https://cyfn.ca/history/history-of-land-claims/.

7   Tramm interview.

8    "An Interview with Sam Johnson," *Voices of Vision: Yukon Aboriginal Self-Government*, Government of Canada, last modified September 2, 2011, https://www.rcaanc-cirnac.gc.ca/eng/1314999952800/1617811084158 <Accessed 20 January 2024>.

9    Liz Hanson, NDP caucus leader and MLA for Whitehorse Centre, author interview, Whitehorse, Yukon, June 13, 2012.

10   "History of Land Claims," Council of Yukon First Nations, accessed January 21, 2024, https://cyfn.ca/history/history-of-land-claims/.

11   Although this amount of land represents a mere fraction of the traditional territories of Yukon First Nations, the settlement land with subsurface mineral rights is scattered across the entire territory in a patchwork design that ensures extensive Indigenous control over land-use decisions.

12   "Learn about Mining Projects and Yukon First Nations," Government of Yukon, accessed January 22, 2024, https://yukon.ca/en/doing-business/funding-and-support-business/learn-about-mining-projects-and-yukon-first-nations#mineral-rights-on-settlement-land.

13   "History of Land Claims," Council of Yukon First Nations, accessed January 23, 2024, https://cyfn.ca/history/history-of-land-claims/.

14   "An Interview with Lesley McCullough," *Voices of Vision: Yukon Aboriginal Self-Government*, Government of Canada, last modified September 2, 2011, https://www.rcaanc-cirnac.gc.ca/eng/1314986766996/1617811423438.

15   "Yukon Forum," Government of Yukon, accessed January 23, 2024, https://yukon.ca/en/your-government/find-out-what-government-doing/yukon-forum.

16   See section titled "Governance," Kwanlin Dün First Nation, accessed January 23, 2024, https://www.kwanlindun.com/.

17   "Clans," Carcross/Tagish First Nation, accessed January 22, 2024, https://www.ctfn.ca/haa-kusteeyi/clans/.

18   "Government Branches of the Ta'an Kwäch'än Council," Ta'an Kwäch'än Council, accessed January 23, 2024, https://taan.ca/governance/.

19   Ruth Massie, grand chief of the CYFN, author interview, Whitehorse, Yukon, June 5, 2012.

20   Dorothy Frost, information officer, Vuntut Gwitchin First Nation Government, author interview, Whitehorse, Yukon, June 11, 2012.

21   Author interview, Whitehorse, Yukon, June 14, 2012.

22   Massie interview.

23   "An Interview with Doris McLean," *Voices of Vision: Yukon Aboriginal Self-Government*, Government of Canada, last modified September 2, 2011, https://www.rcaanc-cirnac.gc.ca/eng/1314984408599/1617811538742.

## NOTES TO CHAPTER 3

1    Author interview, La Paz, Bolivia, August 26, 2014.

2    For data on population size and GDP per capita, see "Bolivia," World Bank, accessed January 8, 2024, https://data.worldbank.org/country/bolivia?view=chart.

3 The member organizations of the Unity Pact included the United Peasant Workers' Confederation of Bolivia, the Confederation of Indigenous Peoples of Bolivia, the Bolivian Syndicalist Confederation of Colonizers, the Bartolina Sisa National Federation of Peasant Women of Bolivia, and the National Council for Ayllus and Markas of Qullasuyu.

4 The series of elections held between 1978 and 1980, against the backdrop of Bolivia's transition to democracy, saw the rise of a number of Indigenous political parties inspired by an ideology known as *Katarismo*, which blends Marxist analysis with Indigenous rights claims. *Katarismo* derives its name from the legendary Inca-descended revolutionary Túpaj Katari, who was executed in 1781 by the Spaniards (Ticona Alejo 2000). None of the *Katarista* parties received more than 1 per cent of the presidential vote. Bolivia's only other contemporary Indigenous-based party is the Pachakuti Indigenous Movement (Movimiento Indígena Pachakuti, or MIP). The MIP competed against Morales and the MAS in the 2002 national elections, capturing 6 per cent of the vote (Van Cott 2005, 86). In the presidential elections of 2005, the MIP managed to garner only 2.2 per cent of the vote, signalling its demise.

5 Electoral reforms in the 2009–10 period guaranteed gender parity and alternation between men and women for national, sub-national, and even judicial elections. The 2010 gender quota law raised the minimum threshold for candidates fielded by political parties from 30 per cent to 50 per cent women in both the lower and upper houses of the congress, making the Bolivian legislature one of the most gender-equal legislatures in the world (Htun 2016, 39).

6 The text of the 2016–20 National Development Plan is available at http://www.planificacion.gob.bo/pdes/pdes2016-2020.pdf.

7 Author interview, La Paz, Bolivia, August 22, 2014.

8 I'm quoting here from Reinaga's statement at the First International Congress on the Philosophy of Fausto Reinaga, which I attended in La Paz, Bolivia, August 21–4, 2014.

## NOTES TO CHAPTER 4

1 Author interview, Iqaluit, Nunavut, June 10, 2013.

2 In this chapter, I follow the advice of Gregory Younging (2018, 66), who explains that "[the term 'Inuit'] is a collective noun. It means *the people*, so it does not take an article or the qualifier *people*."

3 Amagoalik interview.

4 Tagak Curley, member of the Nunavut Legislative Assembly, author interview, Iqaluit, Nunavut, June 10, 2013

5 A map of IOL in Nunavut can be accessed online at https://www.tunngavik.com/files/2011/03/iolmap.pdf.

6 John Quirke, clerk, Legislative Assembly of Nunavut, author interview, Iqaluit, Nunavut, June 6, 2013.

7 Amagoalik interview.

8 For population data, see "Nunavut Statistics," Nunavut Bureau of Statistics, accessed January 23, 2024, https://www.gov.nu.ca/eia/information/statistics-home.

9    Arthur Yuen, legal counsel and coordinator, NTI, author interview, Iqaluit, Nunavut, June 5, 2013.

10   For more on Simon's background, see "Biography," Governor General of Canada, accessed January 23, 2024, https://www.gg.ca/en/governor-general/governor-general-mary-may-simon/biography.

11   Brian Manning, director of education programs, Nunavut Arctic College, author interview, Iqaluit, Nunavut, June 13, 2013.

12   Curley interview.

13   Author interview, Iqaluit, Nunavut, June 11, 2013.

14   Mike interview.

15   Mike interview.

16   Mike interview.

17   See "Nunavut Devolution," Government of Canada, last modified January 18, 2024, https://www.rcaanc-cirnac.gc.ca/eng/1352471770723/1537900871295.

18   Amagoalik interview.

19   Mike interview.

## NOTES TO CHAPTER 5

1    Author interview, Quito, Ecuador, August 29, 2012.

2    For data on population size, see "Ecuador," World Bank, accessed March 15, 2024, https://data.worldbank.org/country/ecuador?view=chart.

3    Indigenous populations in Latin America are notoriously difficult to estimate accurately given the fluid and ambiguous nature of Indigenous identities in the region as well as the technical complexities involved. For data relevant to the Ecuadorian case, see "Indigenous Peoples in Ecuador," International Work Group for Indigenous Affairs, accessed March 15, 2024, https://www.iwgia.org/en/ecuador.html.

4    *Pachakutik* is a Quechua word that means "time for transformation" or the "overturning of order" (Quispe Quispe 2003, 3).

5    Author interview, Quito, Ecuador, August 27, 2012.

6    Ninfa Patiño, analyst, Subsecretary of Interculturality, author interview, Quito, Ecuador, August 23, 2012.

7    Ecuador's National Plan for Living Well (2013–17) is available online at https://www.gobiernoelectronico.gob.ec/wp-content/uploads/2018/10/Plan-Nacional-para-el-Buen-Vivir-2013-%E2%80%93-2017.pdf.

8    Germán Guerra Terán, analyst, Subsecretary of Decentralization, author interview, Quito, Ecuador, August 30, 2012.

9    Antuni interview; Tenesaca interview.

10   Mauricio López, master's student, FLACSO-Ecuador, author interview, Quito, Ecuador, August 20, 2012.

11   Tenesaca interview.

# References

Abele, Frances, and Michael J. Prince. 2003. "Aboriginal Governance and Canadian Federalism: A To-Do List for Canada." In *New Trends in Canadian Federalism*, edited by François Rocher and Miriam Smith, 135–66. Peterborough, ON: Broadview Press.

———. 2006. "Four Pathways to Aboriginal Self-Government in Canada." *American Review of Canadian Studies* 36 (4): 568–95.

Achtenberg, Emily. 2012. "Bolivia: End of the Road for TIPNIS Consulta." *Rebel Currents*, North American Congress on Latin America, December 13, 2012. https://nacla.org/blog/2012/12/13/Bolivia-end-road-tipnis-consulta.

Acosta, Alberto. 2009. "El Estado Plurinacional, Puerta para una Sociedad Democrática: A Manera de Prólogo." In *Plurinacionalidad: Democracia en la Diversidad*, edited by Alberto Acosta and Esperanza Martínez, 15–20. Quito: Ediciones Abya-Yala.

Aglok MacDonald, Stacey. 2009. "Letter from the Youth." In *Staking the Claim: Dreams, Democracy and Canadian Inuit: A Teachers' Guide*, edited by the Nunavut Department of Education, vii–viii. Iqaluit: Government of Nunavut.

AIN (Andean Information Network). 2011. "Turning Point for Morales: Bolivian Police Repress and Detain Indigenous Marchers." Andean Information Network, September 26, 2011. https://ain-bolivia.org/2011/09/turning-point-for-morales-bolivian-police-repress-and-detain-indigenous-marchers/.

Albó, Xavier. 2002. *Pueblos Indios en la Política*. La Paz: Centro de Investigación y Promoción del Campesinado.

———. 2010. "Las Flamantes Autonomías Indígenas en Bolivia." In *La Autonomía a Debate: Autogobierno Indígena y Estado Plurinacional en América Latina*, edited by Miguel González, Araceli Burguete Cal y Mayor, and Pablo Ortiz-T., 355–87. Quito: Facultad Latinoamericana de Ciencias Sociales—Ecuador.

Alcantara, Christopher. 2007. "To Treaty or Not to Treaty? Aboriginal Peoples and Comprehensive Land Claims Negotiations in Canada." *Publius: The Journal of Federalism* 38 (2): 343–69.

———. 2013. *Negotiating the Deal: Comprehensive Land Claims Agreements in Canada*. Toronto: University of Toronto Press.

Alfred, Taiaiake. 2005. *Wasáse: Indigenous Pathways of Action and Freedom*. Toronto: Broadview Press.

———. 2009. *Peace, Power, Righteousness: An Indigenous Manifesto*. New York: Oxford University Press.

Altamirano-Jiménez, Isabel. 2012. *Indigenous Encounters with Neoliberalism: Place, Women, and the Environment in Canada and Mexico.* Vancouver: UBC Press.

Altmann, Philipp. 2016. " 'The Right to Self-Determination': Right and Laws between Means of Oppression and Means of Liberation in the Discourse of the Indigenous Movement of Ecuador." *International Journal for the Semiotics of Law* 29:121–34.

Aks, Judith H. 2004. *Women's Rights in Native North America: Legal Mobilization in the US and Canada.* New York: LFB Scholarly Publishing.

Anaya, James. 2011. "Statement by James Anaya, Special Rapporteur on the Rights of Indigenous Peoples, 66th Session of the General Assembly, Third Committee, 17 October 2011, New York." Jamesanaya.org. Accessed January 14, 2024. https://unsr.jamesanaya.org/?p=559.

Anria, Santiago. 2016. "More Inclusion, Less Liberalism in Bolivia." *Journal of Democracy* 27 (3): 99–108.

———. 2019. *When Movements Become Parties: The Bolivian MAS in Comparative Perspective.* New York: Cambridge University Press.

Aragón, Fernando M. 2015. "The Effect of First Nations Modern Treaties on Local Income." C. D. Howe Institute, E-Brief, October 28, 2015. https://www.cdhowe.org/public-policy-research/effect-first-nations-modern-treaties-local-income.

Arce, Moisés, and Camilo Nieto-Matiz. 2024. "Mining and Violence in Latin America: The State's Coercive Response to Anti-mining Resistance." *World Development* 173 (January): 106404. https://doi.org/10.1016/j.worlddev.2023.106404.

Arce, Moisés, and Roberta Rice. 2009. "Societal Protest in Post-stabilization Bolivia." *Latin American Research Review* 44 (1): 88–101.

Arsel, Murat. 2012. "Between 'Marx' and 'Markets'? The State, The 'Left Turn' and Nature in Ecuador." *Tijdschrift voor Economische en Sociale Geografie* 103 (2): 150–63.

Arteaga Böhrt, Ana Cecilia. 2023. "Gender Orders and Technologies in the Context of Totora Marka's Autonomous Project (Bolivia)." In *Indigenous Territorial Autonomy and Self-Government in the Diverse Americas*, edited by Miguel González, Ritsuko Funaki, Araceli Burguete Cal y Major, José Marimán, and Pablo Ortiz-T., 485–518. Calgary: University of Calgary Press.

Asch, Michael, John Borrows, and James Tully, eds. 2018. *Resurgence and Reconciliation: Indigenous-Settler Relations and Earth Teachings.* Toronto: University of Toronto Press.

Barié, Cletus Gregor. 2022. "Representation of Indigenous Peoples in Times of Progressive Governments: Lessons Learned from Bolivia." *Latin American and Caribbean Ethnic Studies* 17 (2): 167–92.

Barker, Adam J. 2012. "Already Occupied: Indigenous Peoples, Settler Colonialism and the Occupy Movements in North America." *Social Movement Studies* 11 (3–4): 327–34.

Barrera, Anna. 2012. "Turning Legal Pluralism into State-Sanctioned Law: Assessing the Implications of the New Constitutions and Laws in Bolivia and Ecuador." In *New

*Constitutionalism in Latin America: Promises and Practices*, edited by Detlef Nolte and Almut Schilling-Vacaflor, 371–90. Burlington, VT: Ashgate.

Beatriz Ruiz, Carmen. 2007. "Between Paradoxes and Challenges: Promoting Citizenship in Bolivia." In *Citizenship in Latin America*, edited by Joseph S. Tulchin and Meg Ruthenburg, 199–218. Boulder, CO: Lynne Rienner.

Becker, Marc. 2008. *Indians and Leftists in the Making of Ecuador's Modern Indigenous Movements*. Durham, NC: Duke University Press.

———. 2011. *Pachakutik: Indigenous Movements and Electoral Politics in Ecuador*. Lanham, MD: Rowman and Littlefield.

Belanger, Yale D. 2008. "Future Prospects for Aboriginal Self-Government in Canada." In *Aboriginal Self-Government in Canada: Current Trends and Issues*, 3rd ed., edited by Yale D. Belanger, 395–414. Saskatoon: Purich Publishing.

———. 2014. *Ways of Knowing: An Introduction to Native Studies in Canada*, 2nd ed. Toronto: Nelson.

Belanger, Yale D., and David R. Newhouse. 2008. "Reconciling Solitudes: A Critical Analysis of the Self-Government Ideal." In *Aboriginal Self-Government in Canada: Current Trends and Issues*, 3rd ed., edited by Yale D. Belanger, 1–19. Saskatoon: Purich Publishing.

Bengoa, José. 2000. *La Emergencia Indígena en América Latina*. Santiago de Chile: Fondo de Cultura Económica.

Bernauer, Warren. 2019a. "Land Rights and Resource Conflicts in Nunavut." *Polar Geography* 42 (4): 253–66.

———. 2019b. "The Limits to Extraction: Mining and Colonialism in Nunavut." *Canadian Journal of Development Studies* 40 (3): 404–22.

Blackburn, Carole. 2007. "Producing Legitimacy: Reconciliation and the Negotiation of Aboriginal Rights in Canada." *Journal of the Royal Anthropological Institute* 13 (3): 621–38.

Bonifaz, Carlos Romero. 2004. "Las Jornadas de Octubre: Levantamiento Popular en Bolivia." *Artículo Primero: Revista de Debate Social y Jurídico* 8 (16): 13–38.

Borja, Danilo, and Conny Davidsen. 2018. "Can the Yasuní Be Protected through Public Consultation?" Latin American Research Centre, University of Calgary, January 2018. https://larc.ucalgary.ca/publications/new-talk-about-yasuni-public-consultation-and-prospects.

Borrows, John. 2002. *Recovering Canada: The Resurgence of Indigenous Law*. Toronto: University of Toronto Press.

Bosi, Lorenzo, Marco Giugni, and Katrin Uba, eds. 2016. *The Consequences of Social Movements*. New York: Cambridge University Press.

Bretón, Víctor, David Cortez, and Fernando García. 2014. "En Busca del *Sumak Kawsay*: Presentación del Dossier." *Íconos: Revista de Ciencias Sociales* 48:9–24.

Bretón, Víctor, Miguel González, Blanca Rubio, and Leandro Vergara-Camus. 2022. "Peasant and Indigenous Autonomy before and after the Pink Tide in Latin America." *Journal of Agrarian Change* 22 (3): 547–75. https://doi.org/10.1111/joac.12483.

Brinks, Daniel M., Steven Levitsky, and María Victoria Murillo, eds. 2020. *The Politics of Institutional Weakness in Latin America*. New York: Cambridge University Press.

Brooks, Heidi, Trevor Ngwane, and Carin Runciman. 2020. "Decolonising and Re-theorising the Meaning of Democracy: A South African Perspective." *Sociological Review* 68 (1): 17–32.

Cairns, Alan C. 2000. *Citizens Plus: Aboriginal Peoples and the Canadian State*. Vancouver: UBC Press.

Cameron, John. 2009. *Struggles for Local Democracy in the Andes*. Boulder, CO: Lynne Rienner.

Cameron, John, and Wilfredo Plata. 2021. "La Autonomía Indígena en Bolivia: De Grandes Esperanzas a Sueños Desdibujados." In *Autonomías y Autogobierno en la América Diversa*, edited by Miguel González, Araceli Burguete Cal y Mayor, José Marimán, Pablo Ortiz-T., and Ritsuko Funaki, 133–59. Quito: Abya-Yala and Universidad Politécnica Salesiana.

Cameron, Kirk. 2013. "Challenging Free Entry Staking: The Duty to Consult." *Northern Public Affairs* 46:1–3.

Cameron, Kirk, and Graham White. 1995. *Northern Governments in Transition: Political and Constitutional Development in the Yukon, Nunavut, and the Northwest Territories*. Montreal: Institute for Research in Public Policy.

Cameron, Maxwell A. 2014. "New Mechanisms of Democratic Participation in Latin America." *Latin American Studies Association Forum* 45 (1): 4–6.

———. 2018. *Political Institutions and Practical Wisdom: Between Rules and Practice*. New York: Oxford University Press.

Cameron, Maxwell A., Eric Hershberg, and Kenneth E. Sharpe, eds. 2012. *New Institutions for Participatory Democracy in Latin America*. New York: Palgrave Macmillan.

Cameron, Maxwell A., and Kenneth E. Sharpe. 2012. "Institutionalized Voice in Latin American Democracies." In *New Institutions for Participatory Democracy in Latin America*, edited by Maxwell A. Cameron, Eric Hershberg, and Kenneth E. Sharpe, 231–50. New York: Palgrave Macmillan.

Canessa, Andrew. 2012. "Conflict, Claim and Contradiction in the New Indigenous State of Bolivia." desiguALdades.net, Working Paper Series No. 22. https://www.desigualdades.net/Working_Papers/Search-Working-Papers/Working-Paper-22-_Conflict_-Claim-and-Contradiction-in-the-New-Indigenous-State-of-Bolivia_/index.html.

———. 2018. "Indigenous Conflict in Bolivia Explored through an African Lens: Towards a Comparative Analysis of Indigeneity." *Comparative Studies in Society and History* 60 (2): 308–37.

Caria, Sara, and Rafael Domínguez. 2016. "Ecuador's *Buen Vivir*: A New Ideology for Development." *Latin American Perspectives* 43 (1): 18–33.

Castellanos, M. Bianet. 2017. "Introduction: Settler Colonialism in Latin America." *American Quarterly* 69 (4): 777–81.

Centellas, Miguel. 2010. "Bolivia's Regional Elections: A Setback for Evo Morales." *Americas    Quarterly*, April 8, 2010. https://www.americasquarterly.org/article/bolivias-regional-elections-a-setback-for-evo-morales/.

CEPAL (Comisión Económica para América Latina y el Caribe). 2014. *Los Pueblos Indígenas en América Latina: Avances en el Último Decenio y Retos Pendientes para la Garantía de sus Derechos*. Santiago de Chile: United Nations.

Charlie, Lianne Marie Leda. 2020. "Piecing Together Modern Treaty Politics in the Yukon." In *Visions of the Heart: Issues Involving Indigenous Peoples in Canada*, edited by Gina Starblanket and David Long with Olive Patricia Dickason, 83–93. New York: Oxford University Press.

Chartock, Sarah. 2013. " 'Corporatism with Adjectives'? Conceptualizing Civil Society Incorporation and Indigenous Participation in Latin America." *Latin American Politics and Society* 55 (2): 52–76.

Chasteen, John Charles. 2011. *Born in Blood and Fire: A Concise History of Latin America*, 3rd ed. New York: W. W. Norton.

CIPCA (Centro de Investigación y Promoción del Campesinado). 2009. *Posibles Caminos Hacia las Autonomías Indígena Originario Campesinas*. La Paz: CIPCA.

Clapperton, Jonathan, and Liza Piper, eds. 2019. *Environmental Activism on the Ground: Small Green and Indigenous Organizing*. Calgary: University of Calgary Press.

Clarke, Susan E. 2017. "Local Place-Based Collaborative Governance: Comparing State-Centric and Society-Centered Models." *Urban Affairs Review* 53 (3): 578–602.

Coates, Ken S., and W. R. Morrison. 2008. "From Panacea to Reality: The Practicalities of Canadian Aboriginal Self-Government Agreements." In *Aboriginal Self-Government in Canada: Current Trends and Issues*, 3rd ed., edited by Yale D. Belanger, 105–22. Saskatoon: Purich Publishing.

———. 2017. *Land of the Midnight Sun: A History of the Yukon*, 3rd ed. Montreal: McGill-Queen's University Press.

Collier, David. 1995. "Trajectory of a Concept: 'Corporatism' in the Study of Latin American Politics." In *Latin America in Comparative Perspective*, edited by Peter H. Smith, 135–62. Boulder, CO: Westview Press.

Collier, David, and James E. Mahon. 1993. "Conceptual 'Stretching' Revisited: Adapting Categories in Comparative Analysis." *American Political Science Review* 87 (4): 845–55.

Collier, David, and James Mahoney. 1996. "Insights and Pitfalls: Selection Bias in Qualitative Research." *World Politics* 49 (1): 56–91.

Collier, Ruth Berins, and David Collier. 2002. *Shaping the Political Arena: Critical Junctures, the Labor Movement, and Regime Dynamics in Latin America*, 2nd ed. Notre Dame, IN: University of Notre Dame Press.

Collins, Jennifer. 2000. "Una Transición desde las Elites hasta una Democracia Participativa: Apuntes sobre el Papel Emergente de los Movimientos Sociales en el Ecuador." In *Los Movimientos Sociales en las Democracias Andinas*, edited by Julie Massal and Marcelo Bonilla, 55–71. Quito: Facultad Latinoamericana de Ciencias Sociales—Ecuador.

———. 2004. "Linking Movement and Electoral Politics: Ecuador's Indigenous Movement and the Rise of Pachakutik." In *Politics in the Andes: Identity, Conflict, Reform*, edited by Jo-Marie Burt and Philip Mauceri, 38–57. Pittsburgh, PA: University of Pittsburgh Press.

Conaghan, Catherine M. 2008. "Ecuador: Correa's Plebiscitary Presidency." *Journal of Democracy* 19 (2): 46–60.

Cook, Curtis, and Juan D. Lindau, eds. 2000. *Aboriginal Rights and Self-Government: The Canadian and Mexican Experience in North American Perspective*. Montreal: McGill-Queen's University Press.

Corntassel, Jeff, and Cindy Holder. 2008. "Who's Sorry Now? Government Apologies, Truth Commissions, and Indigenous Self-Determination in Australia, Canada, Guatemala, and Peru." *Human Rights Review* 9 (4): 465–89.

Coulthard, Glen Sean. 2014. *Red Skin, White Masks: Rejecting the Colonial Politics of Recognition*. Minneapolis: University of Minnesota Press.

CYFN (Council of Yukon First Nations). 2005. *Constitutional Commission: Final Report and Recommendations*. Whitehorse: CYFN.

———. 2010. *Strategic Plan 2011–2012*. Whitehorse: CYFN.

CYFN and YTG (Yukon Territorial Government). 1997. *Understanding the Yukon Umbrella Agreement: A Land Claim Settlement Information Package*. Whitehorse: CYFN and YTG.

CYI (Council for Yukon Indians). 1973. *Together Today for Our Children Tomorrow: A Statement of Grievances and an Approach to Settlement by the Yukon Indian People*. Whitehorse: CYI.

Danielson, Michael S., and Todd A. Eisenstadt. 2009. "Walking Together, but in Which Direction? Gender Discrimination and Multicultural Practices in Oaxaca, Mexico." *Politics & Gender* 5 (2): 153–84.

De la Torre, Carlos. 2010. "Social Movements and Constituent Processes in Ecuador." In *Challenges to Democratic Governance: Political and Institutional Reforms and Social Movements in the Andean Region*, edited by Martín Tanaka and Francine Jácome, 245–76. Lima: Instituto de Estudios Peruanos.

Della Porta, Donatella. 2013. *Can Democracy Be Saved?* Malden, MA: Polity Press.

Deloria, Vine Jr., and David E. Wilkins. 1999. "Racial and Ethnic Studies, Political Science, and Midwifery." *Wicazo Sa Review* 14 (2): 67–76.

Deneault, Alain, and William Sacher. 2012. *Imperial Canada Inc.: Legal Haven of Choice for the World's Mining Industries.* Vancouver: Talonbooks.

Department of Justice Canada. 2002. *Nunavut Legal Services Study: Final Report.* Ottawa: Government of Canada.

Deruyttere, Anne. 1997. *Indigenous Peoples and Sustainable Development: The Role of the Inter-American Development Bank.* Washington, DC: Inter-American Development Bank.

De Sousa Santos, Boaventura. 2009. "Las Paradojas de Nuestro Tiempo y la Plurinacionalidad." In *Plurinacionalidad: Democracia en al Diversidad*, edited by Alberto Acosta and Esperanza Martínez, 21–62. Quito: Ediciones Abya-Yala.

DIAND (Department of Indian Affairs and Northern Development). 1997. *Nunavut.* Gatineau, QC: DIAND.

Díaz Polanco, Héctor. 1998. "La autonomía, demanda central de los pueblos indígenas: Significado e implicaciones." In *Pueblos Indígenas y Estado en América Latina*, edited by Virginia Alta, Diego Iturralde, and M. A. López Bassola, 213–20. Quito: Ediciones Abya-Yala.

Dosh, Paul, and Nicole Kligerman. 2009. "Correa vs. Social Movements: Showdown in Ecuador." *NACLA Report on the Americas* 42 (5): 21–4.

Drake, Paul W., and Eric Hershberg, eds. 2006. *State and Society in Conflict: Comparative Perspectives on Andean Crises.* Pittsburgh, PA: University of Pittsburgh Press.

Eaton, Kent. 2007. "Backlash in Bolivia: Regional Autonomy as a Reaction against Indigenous Mobilization." *Politics and Society* 35 (1): 71–102.

Eisenstadt, Todd A., and Karleen Jones West. 2019. *Who Speaks for Nature? Indigenous Movements, Public Opinion, and the Petro-State in Ecuador.* New York: Oxford University Press.

Espinosa, Cristina. 2013. "The Riddle of Leaving the Oil in the Soil—Ecuador's Yasuní-ITT Project from a Discourse Perspective." *Forest Policy and Economics* 36:27–36.

Eversole, Robyn. 2010. "Empowering Institutions: Indigenous Lessons and Policy Perils." *Development* 53 (1): 77–82.

Ewig, Christina. 2020. "Ethnic Parties and Indigenous Substantive Representation in Ecuador." *Representation: Journal of Representative Democracy* 58 (3): 391–409.

Exeni Rodríguez, José Luis. 2012. "Elusive Demodiversity in Bolivia: Between Representation, Participation and Self-Government." In *New Institutions for Participatory Democracy in    Latin America*, edited by Maxwell A. Cameron, Eric Hershberg, and Kenneth E. Sharpe,    207–300. New York: Palgrave Macmillan.

Fabricant, Nicole. 2009. "Performative Politics: The Camba Countermovement in Eastern Bolivia." *American Ethnologist* 36 (4): 768–83.

Faguet, Jean-Paul. 2014. "Can Subnational Autonomy Strengthen Democracy in Bolivia?" *Publius: The Journal of Federalism* 44 (1): 51–81.

Falleti, Tulia G. 2021. "Invisible to Political Science: Indigenous Politics in a World in Flux." *Journal of Politics* 83 (1): e5–e12.

Farthing, Linda C., and Benjamin H. Kohl. 2014. *Evo's Bolivia: Continuity and Change.* Austin: University of Texas Press.

Ferguson, Kennan. 2006. "Why Does Political Science Hate American Indians?" *Perspectives on Politics* 14 (4): 1029–38.

Figueroa Romero, Dolores, and Laura Hernández Pérez. 2023. "Autonomy, Intersectionality and Gender Justice: From the 'Double Gaze' of the Women Elders to the Violence We Do Not Know How to Name." In *Indigenous Territorial Autonomy and Self-Government in the Diverse Americas,* edited by Miguel González, Ritsuko Funaki, Araceli Burguete Cal y Major, José Marimán, and Pablo Ortiz-T., 353–85. Calgary: University of Calgary Press.

Fischer, Valdi, and Marc Fasol. 2013. *Las Semillas de "Buen Vivir": La Respuesta de los Pueblos Indígenas del Abya-Yala a la Deriva del Modelo de Desarrollo Occidental.* Quito: Ediciones Fondo Indígena.

Forrest, Maura. 2016. "A Cheque for $69: Yukon First Nations Seek Better Resource Royalty Deal." *Yukon News,* November 23, 2016. https://www.yukon-news. com/news/a-cheque-for-69-yukon-first-nations-seek-better-resource-royalty-deal-6992511.

Fred, Joseph. n.d. "Yukon First Nation Community Profiles." Tr'ondëk Hwëch'in First Nation. Accessed January 14, 2024. https://yukon.ca/sites/yukon.ca/files/ybs/ybs-forms/fin-trondek-hwechin-census-2006.pdf.

Fregoso, Rosa-Linda, and Cynthia Bejarano, eds. 2009. *Terrorizing Women: Feminicide in the Americas.* Durham, NC: Duke University Press.

Frideres, James. 2008. "A Critical Analysis of the Royal Commission on Aboriginal Peoples Self-Government Model." In *Aboriginal Self-Government in Canada,* edited by Yale D. Belanger, 123–44. Saskatoon: Purich Publishing.

Fuentes, Claudio, and Macarena Sánchez. 2018. "Asientos Reservados para Pueblos Indígenas: Experiencia Comparada." Centro de Estudios Interculturales e Indígenas, Policy Papers Series No. 1. https://www.ciir.cl/ciir.cl/wp-content/uploads/2018/07/policy-paper-UPP-n%C2%BA1-2018-1.pdf.

*Gaceta Oficial del Estado Plurinacional de Bolivia.* 2012. No. 0405, August 3, 2012.

Gamarra, Eduardo A. 1994. "Crafting Political Support for Stabilization: Political Pacts and the New Economic Policy in Bolivia." In *Democracy, Markets, and Structural Reform in Latin America,* edited by William C. Smith, Carlos H. Acuña, and Eduardo A. Gamarra, 105–27. Miami: University of Miami, North-South Center.

———. 2008. "Bolivia: Evo Morales and Democracy." In *Constructing Democratic Governance in Latin America,* edited by Jorge I. Domínguez and Michael Shifter, 124–51. Baltimore: Johns Hopkins University Press.

Gamarra, Eduardo, and James M. Malloy. 1995. "The Patrimonial Dynamics of Party Politics in Bolivia." In *Building Democratic Institutions: Party Systems in Latin*

*America*, edited by Scott Mainwaring and Timothy R. Scully, 399–433. Stanford, CA: Stanford University Press.

García Del Moral, Paulina. 2018. "The Murders of Indigenous Women in Canada as Feminicides: Toward a Decolonial Intersectional Reconceptualization of Femicide." *Signs: Journal of Women in Culture and Society* 43 (4): 929–54.

García Linera, Alvaro. 2014. *Identidad Boliviana: Nación, Mestizaje y Plurinacionalidad.* La Paz: Vicepresidencia del Estado Plurinacional.

Gargarella, Roberto. 2013. *Latin American Constitutionalism 1810–2010: The Engine Room of the Constitution.* New York: Oxford University Press.

George, Alexander L., and Andrew Bennett. 2005. *Case Studies and Theory Development in the Social Sciences.* Cambridge, MA: MIT Press.

George, Jane. 2010. "Canada Says Sorry to High Arctic Exiles." *Nunatsiaq News*, August 18, 2010. https://nunatsiaq.com/stories/article/1808101_canada_says_its_sorry_to_the_high_arctic_exiles/.

Gerlach, Allen. 2003. *Indians, Oil, and Politics: A Recent History of Ecuador.* Wilmington, DE: Scholarly Resources.

González, Miguel. 2015. "Indigenous Territorial Autonomy in Latin America: An Overview." *Latin American and Caribbean Ethnic Studies* 10 (1): 10–36.

González, Miguel, Araceli Burguete Cal y Mayor, José Marimán, Pablo Ortiz-T., and Ritsuko Funaki, eds. 2021. *Autonomías y Autogobierno en la América Diversa.* Quito: Ediciones Abya-Yala. English translation (2023): *Indigenous Territorial Autonomy and Self-Government in the Diverse Americas.* Calgary: University of Calgary Press. https://ucp.manifoldapp.org/projects/9781773854632.

Gott, Richard. 2007. "The 2006 SLAS Lecture: Latin America as a White Settler Society." *Bulletin of Latin American Research* 26 (2): 269–89.

Graham, John, Bruce Amos, and Tim Plumptre. 2003. *Principles for Good Governance in the 21st Century.* Policy Brief No. 15. Ottawa: Institute on Governance.

Gudynas, Eduardo. 2011. "Buen Vivir: Today's Tomorrow." *Development* 54 (4): 441–7.

Guérin, Daniel. 2003. "Aboriginal Participation in Canadian Federal Elections: Trends and Implications." *Electoral Insight* 5 (3): 10–15.

Guimont Marceau, Stéphane, Dolores Figueroa Romero, Vivian Jiménez Estrada, and Roberta Rice. 2020. "Approaching Violence against Indigenous Women in the Americas from Relational, Intersectional and Multiscalar Perspectives." *Canadian Journal of Latin American and Caribbean Studies* 45 (1): 5–25.

Gustafson, Bret. 2008. "By Means Legal and Otherwise: The Bolivian Right Regroups." *NACLA Report on the Americas* 41 (1): 20–6.

Gutiérrez Rojas, Moisés. 2003. "Revertir Más de 500 Años de Historia Colonial." In *Los Andes desde Los Andes*, edited by Esteban Ticona Alejo, 171–88. La Paz: Ediciones Yachaywasi.

Hale, Charles R. 2002. "Does Multiculturalism Menace? Governance, Cultural Rights, and the Politics of Identity in Guatemala." *Journal of Latin American Studies* 34 (2): 485–524.

———. 2011. "*Resistencia para que?* Territory, Autonomy and Neoliberal Entanglements in the 'Empty Spaces' of Central America." *Economy and Society* 40 (2): 184–210.

Hart, Ramsey, and Dawn Hoogeveen. 2012. "Introduction to the Legal Framework for Mining in Canada." Working Paper, Mining Watch Canada, July 18, 2012. https://www.miningwatch.ca/2012/7/18/introduction-legal-framework-mining-canada.

Helwig, Maggie. 2017. "Reflecting on Reconciliation." In *Flowers in the Wall: Truth and Reconciliation in Timor-Leste, Indonesia, and Melanesia*, edited by David Webster, 299–308. Calgary: University of Calgary Press.

Henderson, Ailsa. 2007. *Nunavut: Rethinking Political Culture.* Vancouver: UBC Press.

———. 2008. "Self-Government in Nunavut." In *Aboriginal Self-Government in Canada: Current Trends and Issues*, edited by Yale D. Belanger, 222–39. Saskatoon: Purich Publishing.

———. 2009. "Lessons for Social Science in the Study of New Polities: Nunavut at 10." *Journal of Canadian Studies* 43 (2): 5–22.

Hernández Castillo, Rosalva Aída, and Shannon Speed, eds. 2006. *Dissident Women: Gender and Cultural Politics in Chiapas.* Austin: University of Texas Press.

Herrera Acuña, María Fernanda. 2021. "Ley Marco de Autonomía y Descentralización para AIOC: ¿Normatividad Autonómica o Restricción Institucional?" In *Autonomías y Autogobierno en la América Diversa*, edited by Miguel González, Araceli Burguete Cal y Mayor, José Marimán, Pablo Ortiz-T., and Ritsuko Funaki, 111–31. Quito: Abya-Yala and Universidad Politécnica Salesiana.

Hicks, Jack, and Graham White. 2015. *Made in Nunavut: An Experiment in Decentralized Government.* Vancouver: UBC Press.

Hilborn, Paul J. 2014. "Can a State Decolonize Itself? A Critical Analysis of Bolivia's State-Led Decolonization Process." Master's thesis, Dalhousie University.

Htun, Mala, and Juan Pablo Ossa. 2013. "Political Inclusion of Marginalized Groups: Indigenous Reservations and Gender Parity in Bolivia." *Politics, Groups and Identities* 1 (1): 4–25.

Huntington, Samuel P. 1972. *Political Order in Changing Societies.* New Haven, CT: Yale University Press.

INAC (Indian and Northern Affairs Canada). 2008. *Canada's Relationship with Inuit: A History of Policy and Program Development.* Ottawa: INAC.

IQ (Inuit Quajimajatuqanginnut) Task Force. 2002. *The First Annual Report of the Inuit Quajimajatuqanginnut Task Force.* Iqaluit: Government of Nunavut.

Jaramillo, Grace. 2018. "Ecuador Struggles with Rafael Correa's Legacy: The 2018 Referendum and Aftermath." Flash report, Centre for the Study of Democratic Institutions, University of British Columbia, April 2018. https://democracy-network.sites.olt.ubc.ca/files/2018/05/Ecuador-Flash-V4.pdf.

Jensen, Marilyn. 2005. "Institutional Capacity and Financial Viability Relating to Council of Yukon First Nations." In *Constitutional Commission: Background Papers*, edited by CYFN, 45–56. Whitehorse: CYFN.

Keeling, Arn, and John Sandlos. 2015. "Introduction: The Complex Legacy of Mining in Northern Canada." In *Mining and Communities in Northern Canada: History, Politics, and Memory*, edited by Arn Keeling and John Sandlos, 1–32. Calgary: University of Calgary Press.

Keme, Emil. 2018. "For Abiayala to Live, the Americas Must Die: Towards a Transhemispheric Indigeneity." *Native American and Indigenous Studies* 5 (1): 42–68.

Kohl, Benjamin. 2002. "Stabilizing Neoliberalism in Bolivia: Popular Participation and Privatization." *Political Geography* 21 (4): 449–72.

Kohl, Benjamin, and Linda Farthing. 2006. *Impasse in Bolivia: Neoliberal Hegemony and Popular Resistance*. London: Zed Books.

Kohli, Atul, Peter Evans, Peter J. Katzenstein, Adam Przeworski, Susanne Hoeber Rudolph, James C. Scott, and Theda Skocpol. 1996. "The Role of Theory in Comparative Politics: A Symposium." *World Politics* 48 (1): 1–49.

Komadina, Jorge. 2016. "Paradojas de la Representación Política en Bolivia." *L'Âge d'or* 9:1–15.

Kovach, Margaret Elizabeth. 2000. *Indigenous Methodologies: Characteristics, Conversations, and Contexts*. Toronto: University of Toronto Press.

Krahmann, Elke. 2003. "National, Regional, and Global Governance: One Phenomenon or Many?" *Global Governance* 9 (3): 323–46.

Kuokkanen, Rauna. 2019. *Restructuring Relations: Indigenous Self-Determination, Governance, and Gender*. New York: Oxford University Press.

Ladner, Kiera. 2003. "The Alienation of Nation: Understanding Aboriginal Electoral Participation." *Electoral Insight* 5 (3): 21–6.

———. 2018. "Proceed with Caution: Reflections on Resurgence and Reconciliation." In *Resurgence and Reconciliation: Indigenous-Settler Relations and Earth Teachings*, edited by Michael Asch, John Borrows, and James Tully, 245–64. Toronto: University of Toronto Press.

Ladner, Kiera, and Michael Orsini. 2003. "The Persistence of Paradigm Paralysis: The *First Nations Governance Act* as the Continuation of Colonial Policy." In *Reconfiguring Aboriginal-State Relations*, edited by Michael Murphy, 185–203. Montreal: McGill-Queen's University Press.

Lalander, Rickard. 2014. "Rights of Nature and the Indigenous Peoples in Bolivia and Ecuador: A Straitjacket for Progressive Development Politics?" *Iberoamerican Journal of Development Studies* 3 (2): 148–73.

Lalander, Rickard, and Magnus Lembke. 2020. "Interculturality from Below: Territoriality and Floating Indigenous Identities in Plurinational Ecuador." *Ciencias Políticas y Relaciones Internacionales* 9 (1): 129–58.

Lalander, Rickard, Magnus Lembke, and Pablo Ospina Peralta. 2019. "Political Economy of State-Indigenous Liaisons: Ecuador in Times of Alianza PAIS." *European Review of Latin American and Caribbean Studies* 108:193–220.

Larson, Brooke. 2004. *Trials of Nation Making: Liberalism, Race, and Ethnicity in the Andes, 1810–1910.* New York: Cambridge University Press.

Laserna, Roberto. 2002. "Conflictos Sociales y Movimientos Políticos en Bolivia." In *Las Piedras en el Camino: Movimientos Sociales del 2000 en Bolivia*, edited by María Lujan Veneros, 7–38. La Paz: Ministerio de Desarrollo Sostenible y Planificación.

Layton, Heather Marie, and Harry Anthony Patrinos. 2006. "Estimating the Number of Indigenous Peoples in Latin America." In *Indigenous Peoples, Poverty and Human Development in Latin America, 1994–2004*, edited by Gillette Hall and Harry Anthony Patrinos, 25–39. New York: Palgrave Macmillan.

Légaré, André. 2008. "Canada's Experiment with Aboriginal Self-Determination in Nunavut: From Vision to Illusion." *International Journal on Minority and Group Rights* 15 (2–3): 335–67.

Levi-Faur, David. 2012. "From 'Big Government' to 'Big Governance.'" In *Oxford Handbook of Governance*, edited by David Levi-Faur, 3–18. New York: Oxford University Press.

Levitsky, Steven. 2012. "Informal Institutions and Politics in Latin America." In *Routledge Handbook of Latin American Politics*, edited by Peter Kingstone and Deborah J. Yashar, 88–100. New York: Routledge.

Levitsky, Steven, and Kenneth M. Roberts. 2011. "Conclusion: Democracy, Development, and the Left." In *The Resurgence of the Latin America Left*, edited by Steven Levitsky and Kenneth M. Roberts, 399–428. Baltimore: Johns Hopkins University Press.

Lindau, Juan D., and Curtis Cook. 2000. "One Continent, Contrasting Styles: The Canadian Experience in North American Perspective." In *Aboriginal Rights and Self-Government: The Canadian and Mexican Experience in North American Perspective*, edited by Curtis Cook and Juan D. Lindau, 3–36. Montreal: McGill-Queen's University Press.

Lindt, Angela. 2023. "The Dark Side of Judicialization: Criminalizing Mining Protests in Peru." *Latin American Research Review* 58 (2): 368–82.

Lucas, Kintto. 2000. *La Rebelión de los Indios.* Quito: Ediciones Abya-Yala.

Lucero, José Antonio. 2008. *Struggles of Voice: The Politics of Indigenous Representation in the Andes.* Pittsburgh, PA: University of Pittsburgh Press.

———. 2012. "Indigenous Politics: Between Democracy and Danger." In *Routledge Handbook of Latin American Politics*, edited by Peter Kingstone and Deborah J. Yashar, 285–301. New York: Routledge.

———. 2013. "Ambivalent Multiculturalisms: Perversity, Futility, and Jeopardy in Latin America." In *Latin America's Multicultural Movements: The Struggle between Communitarianism, Autonomy, and Human Rights*, edited by Todd A. Eisenstadt,

Michael S. Danielson, Moisés Jaime Bailón Corres, and Carlos Sorroza Polo, 18–39. New York: Oxford University Press.

Lupien, Pascal. 2016. " 'Radical' Participatory Democracy Institutions in Venezuela and Ecuador: Strengthening Civil Society or Mechanisms for Controlled Inclusion?" In *Re-imagining Community and Civil Society in Latin America and the Caribbean*, edited by Gordana Yovanovich and Roberta Rice, 197–217. New York: Routledge.

Maaka, Roger, and Augie Fleras. 2005. *The Politics of Indigeneity: Challenging the State in Canada and Aotearoa New Zealand*. Dunedin, NZ: University of Otago Press.

Macas, Luis. 2009. "Construyendo desde la Historia: Resistencia del Movimiento Indígena en el Ecuador." In *Plurinacionalidad: Democracia en la Diversidad*, edited by Alberto Acosta and Esperanza Martínez, 81–98. Quito: Ediciones Abya-Yala.

MacDonald, Brian L. 2005. "Intergovernmental Relations: Aboriginal and Non-Aboriginal Governments." In *Constitutional Commission: Background Papers*, edited by CYFN, 29–44. Whitehorse: CYFN.

Madrid, Raúl L. 2012. *The Rise of Ethnic Politics in Latin America*. New York: Cambridge University Press.

Mainwaring, Scott P. 1999. *Rethinking Party Systems in the Third Wave of Democratization: The Case of Brazil*. Stanford, CA: Stanford University Press.

Mainwaring, Scott, and Timothy R. Scully. 1995. "Introduction." In *Building Democratic Institutions: Party Systems in Latin America*, edited by Scott Mainwaring and Timothy R. Scully, 1–34. Stanford, CA: Stanford University Press.

March, James, and Johan P. Olsen. 1989. *Rediscovering Institutions: The Organizational Basis of Politics*. New York: Free Press.

Martínez, Ignacio. 2016. "Settler Colonialism in New Spain and the Early Mexican Republic." In *The Routledge Handbook of the History of Settler Colonialism*, edited by Edward Cavanagh and Lorenzo Veracini, 109–24. New York: Routledge.

Martínez Novo, Carmen. 2014. "Managing Diversity in Postneoliberal Ecuador." *Journal of Latin American and Caribbean Anthropology* 19 (1): 103–25.

———. 2021. *Undoing Multiculturalism: Resource Extraction and Indigenous Rights in Ecuador*. Pittsburgh, PA: University of Pittsburgh Press.

Massal, Julie, and Marcelo Bonilla. 2000. "Introducción: Movimientos Sociales, Democracia y Cambio Socio-Político en el Area Andina." In *Los Movimientos Sociales en las Democracias Andinas*, edited by Julie Massal and Marcelo Bonilla, 7–38. Quito: Facultad Latinoamericana de Ciencias Sociales—Ecuador.

McComber, Louis, ed. 2007. *John Amagoalik: Changing the Face of Canada*. Iqaluit: Nunavut Arctic College.

McElroy, Ann. 2008. *Nunavut Generations: Change and Continuity in Canadian Inuit Communities*. Long Grove, IL: Waveland Press.

McNeil, Kent. 2001. *Emerging Justice? Essays on Indigenous Rights in Canada and Australia*. Saskatoon: Native Law Centre, University of Saskatchewan.

Mejía Acosta, Andrés, María Caridad Arauja, Aníbal Pérez-Liñán, and Sebastían Saiegh. 2008. "Veto Players, Fickle Institutions, and Low-Quality Policies: The Policymaking Process in Ecuador." In *Policymaking in Latin America: How Politics Shapes Policies*, edited by Ernesto Stein and Mariano Tomassi, 243–85. New York: Inter-American Development Bank.

Merino, Roger. 2021. *Socio-Legal Struggles for Indigenous Self-Determination in Latin America: Reimagining the Nation, Reinventing the State*. New York: Routledge.

Milen, Robert A. 1991. "Aboriginal Constitutional and Electoral Reform." In *Aboriginal Peoples and Electoral Reform in Canada*, edited by Robert A. Millen, 3–65. Toronto: Dundurn Press.

Montúfar, César. 2006. "Representation and Active Citizenship in Ecuador." In *Citizenship in Latin America*, edited by Joseph S. Tulchin and Meg Ruthenburg, 235–49. Boulder, CO: Lynne Rienner.

Morse, Bradford. 2008. "Regaining Recognition of the Inherent Right of Aboriginal Government." In *Aboriginal Self-Government in Canada: Current Trends and Issues*, 3rd ed., edited by Yale D. Belanger, 39–68. Saskatoon: Purich Publishing.

MUPP-NP (Movimiento de Unidad Plurinacional Pachakutik—Nuevo País). 1999. "Primer Congreso Nacional." *El Churo* 2:3–32.

———. 2003. "Unidad, Organización, Interculturalidad para Construir un Nuevo País." *El Churo* 6:1–48.

Nadasdy, Paul. 2003. *Hunters and Bureaucrats: Power, Knowledge, and Aboriginal-State Relations in the Southwest Yukon*. Vancouver: UBC Press.

———. 2005. "The Anti-politics of TEK: The Institutionalization of Co-management Discourse and Practice." *Anthropologica* 47 (2): 215–32.

NIC (Nunavut Implementation Commission). 1995. *Footprints in New Snow: A Comprehensive Report from the Nunavut Implementation Commission to the Department of Indian Affairs and Northern Development, Government of the Northwest Territories and Nunavut Tunngavik Incorporated Concerning the Establishment of the Nunavut Government*. Iqaluit: NIC.

———. 1996. *Footprints 2: A Second Comprehensive Report from the Nunavut Implementation Committee to the Department of Indian Affairs and Northern Development, Government of Northwest Territories and Nunavut Tunngavik Inc. Concerning the Establishment of the Nunavut Government*. Iqaluit: NIC.

North, Douglass C. 1990. *Institutions, Institutional Change and Economic Performance*. New York: Cambridge University Press.

NTI (Nunavut Tunngavik Incorporated). 2009. "Inuit Owned Lands; Mining and Royalty Regimes." NLCA Workshop slides, November 25, 2009. https://www.tunngavik.com/documents/publications/administration/IOL%20and%20Minerals%2025Nov09.pdf.

O'Donnell, Guillermo. 1996. "Illusions about Consolidation." *Journal of Democracy* 7 (2): 34–51.

———. 2010. *Democracy, Agency, and the State: Theory with Comparative Intent*. New York: Oxford University Press.

Olivera, Oscar, and Tom Lewis. 2004. *¡Cochabamba! Water War in Bolivia*. Cambridge: South End Press.

Ortiz-T., Pablo. 2015. "El Laberinto de la Autonomía Indígena en el Ecuador: Las Circunscripciones Territoriales Indígenas en la Amazonía Central, 2010–2012." *Latin American and Caribbean Ethnic Studies* 10 (1): 60–86.

———. 2021. "Autonomía Indígena en Ecuador: Fundamentos, Extravíos y Desafíos." In *Autonomías y Autogobierno en la América Diversa*, edited by Miguel González, Araceli Burguete Cal y Mayor, José Marimán, Pablo Ortiz-T., and Ritsuko Funaki, 439–70. Quito: Ediciones Abya-Yala.

Oxhorn, Philip. 1998. "Is the Century of Corporatism Over? Neoliberalism and the Rise of Neopluralism." In *What Kind of Democracy? What Kind of Market? Latin America in the Age of Neoliberalism*, edited by Philip D. Oxhorn and Graciela Ducatenzeiler, 195–217.    University Park: Pennsylvania University Press.

———. 2011. *Sustaining Civil Society: Economic Change, Democracy and the Social Construction of Citizenship in Latin America*. University Park: Pennsylvania State University Press.

———. 2016. "Civil Society from the Inside Out: Community, Organization and the Challenge of Political Influence." In *Re-imagining Community and Civil Society in Latin America and the Caribbean*, 20–46. New York: Routledge.

Pacari, Nina. 1996. "Taking On the Neoliberal Agenda." *NACLA Report on the Americas* 29 (5): 23–32.

Palmater, Pamela D. 2011. *Beyond Blood: Rethinking Indigenous Identity*. Saskatoon: Purich Publishing.

Papillon, Martin. 2008. "Canadian Federalism and the Emerging Mosaic of Aboriginal Multilevel Governance." In *Canadian Federalism: Performance, Effectiveness and Legitimacy*, 2nd ed., edited by Herman Bakvis and Grace Skogstad, 291–313. New York: Oxford University Press.

Peña y Lillo, Julio E. 2012. "Estado y Movimientos Sociales: Historia de una Dialéctica Impostergable." *Íconos: Revista de Ciencias Sociales* 44:67–83.

Pereira, Ricardo, and Orla Gough. 2013. "Permanent Sovereignty over Natural Resources in the 21st Century: Natural Resource Governance and the Right to Self-Determination of Indigenous Peoples under International Law." *Melbourne Journal of International Law* 14 (2): 451–95.

Peruzzotti, Enrique, and Andrew Selee. 2009. "Participatory Innovation and Representative Democracy in Latin America." In *Participatory Innovation and Representative Democracy in Latin America*, edited by Andrew Selee and Enrique

Peruzzotti, 1–16. Washington, DC: Woodrow Wilson Centre; Baltimore: Johns Hopkins University Press.

Phillips, Tom, and Dan Collyns. 2020. "Bolivia Election: Evo Morales's Leftwing Party Celebrates Stunning Comeback." *The Guardian*, October 19, 2020. https://www. theguardian.com/world/2020/oct/19/bolivia-election-exit-polls-suggest-thumping-win-evo-morales-party-luis-arce.

Picq, Manuela L. 2017. "Indigenous Politics of Resistance: An Introduction." *New Diversities* 19 (2): 1–6.

*Plan de Desarrollo Económico y Social en el Marco Del Desarrollo Integral Para Vivir Bien, 2016–2020.* 2016. La Paz: Estado Plurinacional de Bolivia.

*Plan Nacional para El Buen Vivir, 2013–2017.* 2013. Quito: República del Ecuador.

Platt, Tristan. 1987. "The Andean Experience of Bolivian Liberalism, 1825–1900: Roots of Rebellion in 19th Century Chayanta (Potosí)." In *Resistance, Rebellion, and Consciousness in the Andean Peasant World, 18th to 20th Centuries*, edited by Steven J. Stern, 280–324. Madison: University of Wisconsin Press.

Postero, Nancy Grey. 2007. *Now We Are Citizens: Indigenous Politics in Postmulticultural Bolivia.* Stanford, CA: Stanford University Press.

———. 2017. *The Indigenous State: Race, Politics, and Performance in Plurinational Bolivia.* Oakland: University of California Press.

Postero, Nancy, and Jason Tockman. 2020. "Self-Governance in Bolivia's First Indigenous Autonomy: Charagua." *Latin American Research Review* 55 (1): 1–15.

Prno, Jason. 2013. "An Analysis of Factors Leading to the Establishment of a Social License to Operate in the Mining Industry." *Resources Policy* 38 (4): 577–90.

Quispe Quispe, Eusebio. 2003. "El Indio y la revuelta." *Pachakuti: Vocero Oficial del Movimiento Indígena Pachakuti (MIP)*, March 15, 2003, 3.

Radcliffe, Sarah A. 2012. "Development for a Postneoliberal Era? *Sumak Kawsay*, Living Well and the Limits to Decolonisation in Ecuador." *Geoforum* 43 (2): 240–9.

Radhuber, Isabella M., and Sarah A. Radcliffe. 2022. "Contested Sovereignties: Indigenous Disputes over Plurinational Resource Governance." *Environment and Planning E: Nature and Space* 6 (1). https://doi.org/10.1177/25148486211068476.

Regan, Paulette. 2010. *Unsettling the Settler Within: Indian Residential Schools, Truth Telling, and Reconciliation in Canada.* Vancouver: UBC Press.

Regino Montes, Adelfo, and Gustavo Torres Cisneros. 2009. "The United Nations Declaration on the Rights of Indigenous Peoples: The Foundation of a New Relationship between Indigenous Peoples, States and Societies." In *Making the Declaration Work: The United Nations Declaration on the Rights of Indigenous Peoples*, edited by Claire Charters and Rodolfo Stavenhagen, 138–68. Copenhagen: IWGIA.

Resina de la Fuente, Jorge. 2012. *La Plurinacionalidad en Disputa: El Pulso entre Correa y la CONAIE.* Quito: Ediciones Abya-Yala.

Retolaza Eguren, Iñigo. 2008. "Moving Up and Down the Ladder: Community-Based Participation in Public Dialogue and Deliberation in Bolivia and Guatemala." *Community Development Journal* 43 (3): 312–28.

Rice, Roberta. 2011a. "Bolivia: Ethnicity and Power." In *The Paradox of Democracy in Latin America: Ten Country Studies of Division and Resilience*, edited by Katherine Isbester, 277–98. Toronto: University of Toronto Press.

———. 2011b. "From the Ground Up: The Challenge of Indigenous Party Consolidation in Latin America." *Party Politics* 17 (2): 171–88.

———. 2012. *The New Politics of Protest: Indigenous Mobilization in Latin America's Neoliberal Era*. Tucson: University of Arizona Press.

———. 2014a. "Achieving First Nation Self-Government in Yukon, Canada: The Mediating Role of the Council for Yukon Indians (CYI), 1975–1995." In *Mediated Citizenship: The Informal Politics of Speaking for Citizens in the Global South*, edited by Bettina Von Lieres and Laurence Piper, 203–18. New York: Palgrave Macmillan.

———. 2014b. "UNDRIP and the 2009 Bolivian Constitution: Lessons for Canada." In *Special Report: The Internationalization of Indigenous Rights—UNDRIP in the Canadian Context*, edited by Centre for International Governance Innovation, 59–63. Waterloo, ON: Centre for International Governance Innovation.

———. 2016. "How to Decolonize Democracy: Indigenous Governance Innovation in Bolivia and Nunavut, Canada." *Bolivian Studies Journal* 22:220–42.

———. 2019. "The Politics of Free, Prior and Informed Consent: Indigenous Rights and Resource Governance in Ecuador and Yukon, Canada." *International Journal on Minority and Group Rights* 27 (2): 336–56.

———. 2020a. "Does Indigenous Mainstreaming Work? Mechanisms of Indigenous Interest Representation in Bolivia." *Representation: Journal of Representative Democracy* 58 (3): 411–26.

———. 2020b. "Indigenous Autonomies under the New Left in the Andes." In *Legacies of the Left Turn in Latin America: The Promise of Inclusive Citizenship*, edited by Manuel Balán and Françoise Montambeault, 161–82. Notre Dame, IN: University of Notre Dame Press.

———. 2021. "Two Different Visions of the Left Divide Ecuador in the 2021 Presidential Election." North American Congress on Latin America, February 13, 2021. https://nacla.org/news/2021/02/13/two-different-visions-left-divide-ecuador-2021-presidential-election.

Ritsema, Roger, Jackie Dawson, Miriam Jorgensen, and Brenda Macdougall. 2015. " 'Steering Our Own Ship?' An Assessment of Self-Determination and Self-Governance for Community Development in Nunavut." *Northern Review* 41:157–80.

Rivera Cusicanqui, Silvia. 2020. *Ch'ixinakax Utxiwa: On Practices and Discourses of Decolonization*. Cambridge: Polity Press.

Roberts, Kenneth M. 1998. *Deepening Democracy? The Modern Left and Social Movements in Chile and Peru.* Stanford, CA: Stanford University Press.

———. 2016. "Democracy in the Developing World: Challenges of Survival and Significance." *Studies in Comparative International Development* 51 (1): 32–49.

Rodon, Thierry. 2017. "Institutional Development and Resource Development: The Case of Canada's Indigenous Peoples." *Canadian Journal of Development Studies* 39 (1): 119–36.

Rothstein, Bo. 1996. "Political Institutions: An Overview." In *A New Handbook of Political Science*, edited by Robert E. Goodin and Hans-Dieter Klingemann, 133–66. New York: Oxford University Press.

Rousseau, Stéphanie, and Anahi Morales Hudon. 2017. *Indigenous Women's Movements in Latin America: Gender and Ethnicity in Peru, Mexico, and Bolivia.* New York: Palgrave Macmillan.

Rueschemeyer, Dietrich, Evelyne Huber Stephens, and John D. Stephens. 1992. *Capitalist Development and Democracy.* Chicago: University of Chicago Press.

Saavedra, Alejandro. 2002. *Los Mapuche en la Sociedad Chilena Actual.* Santiago de Chile: LOM Ediciones.

Sabin, Jerald. 2014. "Contested Colonialism: Responsible Government and Political Development in Yukon." *Canadian Journal of Political Science* 47 (2): 375–96.

Sambo Dorough, Dalee. 2021. "El Derecho a la Libre Determinación y los Pueblos Indígenas: La Continue Búsqueda a la Igualdad." In *Autonomías y Autogobierno en la América Diversa*, edited by Miguel González, Araceli Burguete Cal y Mayor, José Marimán, Pablo Ortiz-T., and Ritsuko Funaki, 39–63. Quito: Ediciones Abya-Yala.

Samson, Colin, and Carlos Gigoux. 2016. *Indigenous Peoples and Colonialism: Global Perspectives.* Cambridge: Polity Press.

Sb, Girisanker, and Vrinda Aravind. 2022. "Challenges to Democratic Consolidation in Ecuador—Space for Opposition and Indigenous Representation under Rafael Correa and Lenin Moreno." *Democracy and Security* 18 (1): 51–66.

Schilling-Vacaflor, Almut, and René Kuppe. 2012. "Plurinational Constitutionalism: A New Era of Indigenous-State Relations?" In *New Constitutionalism in Latin America: Promises and Practices*, edited by Detlef Nolte and Almut Schilling-Vacaflor, 347–70. Burlington, VT: Ashgate.

Scholtz, Christa. 2006. *Negotiating Claims: The Emergence of Indigenous Land Claim Negotiation Policies in Australia, Canada, New Zealand, and the United States.* New York: Routledge.

Schulz, Carsten-Andreas. 2018. "Territorial Sovereignty and the End of Inter-cultural Diplomacy along the 'Southern Frontier.' " *European Journal of International Relations* 25 (3): 878–903.

Selverston, Melina. 1997. "The Politics of Identity Reconstruction: Indians and Democracy in Ecuador." In *The New Politics of Inequality in Latin America*, edited by Douglas A. Chalmers, Carlos M. Vilas, Katherine Hite, Scott B. Martin, Kerianne Piester, and Monique Segarra, 170–91. New York: Oxford University Press.

Sieder, Rachel. 2011. "Contested Sovereignties: Indigenous Law, Violence and State Effects in Postwar Guatemala." *Critique of Anthropology* 31 (3): 161–84.

———. 2016. "Indigenous Peoples' Rights and the Law in Latin America." In *Handbook of Indigenous Peoples' Rights*, edited by Corinne Lennox and Damien Short, 414–23. New York: Routledge.

Sieder, Rachel, and Anna Barrera Vivero. 2017. "Legalizing Indigenous Self-Determination: Autonomy and *Buen Vivir* in Latin America." *Journal of Latin American and Caribbean Anthropology* 22 (1): 9–26.

Silva, Eduardo. 2009. *Challenging Neoliberalism in Latin America*. New York: Cambridge University Press.

———, ed. 2013. *Transnational Activism and National Movements in Latin America: Bridging the Divide*. New York: Routledge.

Simpson, Audra. 2014. *Mohawk Interruptus: Political Life across the Borders of Settler States*. Durham, NC: Duke University Press.

Simpson, Leanne Betasamosake. 2017. *As We Have Always Done: Indigenous Freedom through Radical Resistance*. Minneapolis: University of Minnesota Press.

Singh, Jakeet. 2019. "Decolonizing Radical Democracy." *Contemporary Political Theory* 18 (4): 331–56.

Slater, Dan. 2013. "Democratic Careening." *World Politics* 65 (4): 729–63.

Smith, Graham. 2009. *Democratic Innovations: Designing Institutions for Citizen Participation*. New York: Cambridge University Press.

Smith, Linda Tuhiwai. 1999. *Decolonizing Methodologies: Research and Indigenous Peoples*. London: Zed Books.

Soruco Sologuren, Ximena, Daniela Franco Pinto, and Mariela Durán Azurduy. 2014. *Composición Social del Estado Plurinacional: Hacia la Descolonización de la Burocracia*. La Paz: Vicepresidencia del Estado.

Speed, Shannon. 2016. "States of Violence: Indigenous Women Migrants in the Era of Neoliberal Multicriminalism." *Critique of Anthropology* 36 (3): 280–301.

———. 2017. "Structures of Settler Capitalism in Abya Yala." *American Quarterly* 69 (4): 783–90.

Starblanket, Gina. 2020. "Crises of Relationship: The Role of Treaties in Contemporary Indigenous-Settler Relations." In *Visions of the Heart: Issues Involving Indigenous Peoples in Canada*, 5th ed., edited by Gina Starblanket and David Long with Olive Patricia Dickason, 13–33. New York: Oxford University Press.

Stavenhagen, Rodolfo. 2002. "Indigenous Peoples and the State in Latin America: An Ongoing Debate." In *Multiculturalism in Latin America: Indigenous Rights, Diversity and Democracy*, edited by Rachel Sieder, 24–44. New York: Palgrave Macmillan.

Stevenson, Marc G. 2006. "The Possibility of Difference: Rethinking Co-management." *Human Organization* 65 (2): 167–80.

Suárez, Hugo José. 2003. *Una Semana Fundamental: 10–18 Octubre 2003*. La Paz: Muela del Diablo.

Swyngedouw, Erik. 2005. "Governance Innovation and the Citizen: The Janus Face of Governance-beyond-the-State." *Urban Studies* 42 (11): 1991–2006.

Szablowski, David. 2010. "Operationalizing Free, Prior, and Informed Consent in the Extractive Industry Sector? Examining the Challenges of a Negotiated Model of Justice." *Canadian Journal of Development Studies* 30 (1–2): 111–30.

Talpin, Julien. 2015. "Democratic Innovations." In *The Oxford Handbook of Social Movements*, edited by Donatella Della Porta and Mario Diani, 1–16. New York: Oxford University Press.

Tapia, Luís. 2011. "Consideraciones sobre el Estado Plurinacional." In *Descolonización en Bolivia: Cuatro Ejes Para Comprender el Cambio*, edited by Gonzálo Gosálvez and Jorge Dulon, 135–68. La Paz: Vicepresidencia del Estado/Fundación Boliviana para la Democracia Multipartidaria.

Tester, Frank James, and Peter Irniq. 2008. "*Inuit Qaujimajatuqangit*: Social History, Politics and the Practice of Resistance." *Arctic* 61 (1): 48–61.

TFN (Tunngavik Federation of Nunavut). 1992. Internal memo on the Nunavut Lands Claims Agreement. Nunavut Legislative Library collection.

Timpson, Annis May. 2006. "Stretching the Concept of Representative Bureaucracy: The Case of Nunavut." *International Review of Administrative Sciences* 72 (4): 517–30.

———. 2009a. "Reconciling Indigenous and Settler Language Interests: Language Policy Initiatives in Nunavut." *Journal of Canadian Studies* 43 (2): 159–80.

———. 2009b. "Rethinking the Administration of Government: Inuit Representation, Culture, and Language in the Nunavut Public Service." In *First Nations, First Thoughts: The Impact of Indigenous Thought in Canada*, edited by Annis May Timpson, 199–228. Vancouver: UBC Press.

Tockman, Jason. 2006. "Decentralisation, Socio-territoriality and the Exercise of Indigenous Self-Governance in Bolivia." *Third World Quarterly* 37 (1): 153–71.

———. 2017. "The Hegemony of Representation: Democracy and Indigenous Self-Government in Bolivia." *Journal of Politics in Latin America* 9 (2): 121–38.

Tockman, Jason, and John Cameron. 2014. "Indigenous Autonomy and the Contradictions of Plurinationalism in Bolivia." *Latin American Politics and Society* 56 (3): 46–69.

Tockman, Jason, John Cameron, and Wilfredo Plata. 2015. "New Institutions of Indigenous Self-Governance in Bolivia: Between Autonomy and Self-Discipline." *Latin American and Caribbean Ethnic Studies* 10 (1): 37–59.

Tomaselli, Alexandra. 2017. "The Right to Political Participation of Indigenous Peoples: A Holistic Approach." *International Journal on Minority and Group Rights* 24 (4): 390–427.

TRC (Truth and Reconciliation Commission of Canada). 2015. *Honouring the Truth, Reconciling for the Future: Summary of the Final Report of the Truth and*

*Reconciliation Commission of Canada*. Winnipeg: TRC. https://nctr.ca/records/reports/#trc-reports.

"TSE: Los Indígenas Aceptan Vía, Pero Con Condiciones." 2013. *Los Tiempos*, January 8, 2013. https://www.lostiempos.com/actualidad/nacional/20130107/tse-indigenas-aceptan-pero-condiciones.

Tuck, Eve, and K. Wayne Yang. 2012. "Decolonization Is Not a Metaphor." *Decolonization: Indigeneity, Education & Society* 1 (1): 1–40.

Tully, James. 1995. *Strange Multiplicity: Constitutionalism in an Age of Diversity*. New York: Cambridge University Press.

———. 2000. "A Just Relationship between Aboriginal and Non-Aboriginal Peoples of Canada." In *Aboriginal Rights and Self-Government: The Canadian and Mexican Experience in North American Perspective*, edited by Curtis Cook and Juan D. Lindau, 39–71. Montreal: McGill-Queen's University Press.

Turner, Dale. 2006. *This Is Not a Peace Pipe: Towards a Critical Indigenous Philosophy*. Toronto: University of Toronto Press.

Ugalde, Silvia. 2014. "El Orden de Género en El *Sumak Kawsay* y el *Suma Qamaña*. Un Vistazo a los Debates Actuales en Bolivia y Ecuador." *Íconos: Revista de Ciencias Sociales* 48:73–91.

Van Cott, Donna Lee. 2000. *The Friendly Liquidation of the Past: The Politics of Diversity in Latin America*. Pittsburgh, PA: University of Pittsburgh Press.

———. 2005. *From Movements to Parties in Latin America: The Evolution of Ethnic Politics*. New York: Cambridge University Press.

———. 2008. *Radical Democracy in the Andes*. New York: Cambridge.

———. 2009. "Indigenous Movements Lose Momentum." *Current History* 108 (715): 83–9.

Vanden, Harry E., and Gary Prevost. 2009. *Politics of Latin America: The Power Game*, 3rd ed. New York: Oxford University Press.

Van den Hoonaard, Deborah K. 2015. *Qualitative Research in Action: A Canadian Primer*, 3rd ed. New York: Oxford University Press.

Veltmeyer, Henry. 2007. *On the Move: The Politics of Social Change in Latin America*. Toronto: University of Toronto Press.

Veracini, Lorenzo. 2016. "Introduction: Settler Colonialism as a Distinct Mode of Domination." In *The Routledge Handbook of the History of Settler Colonialism*, edited by Edward Cavanagh and Lorenzo Veracini, 1–8. New York: Routledge.

Vice Ministerio de Descolonización. 2013. *Resoluciones: 1ra Cumbre Internacional de Descolonización, Despatriarcalización, Lucha Contra el Racismo y la Discriminación*. La Paz: Ministerio de Culturas y Turismo.

———. 2014. *Descolonizando el Estado desde El Estado*. La Paz: Ministerio de Culturas y Turismo.

Wade, Peter. 2010. *Race and Ethnicity in Latin America*, 2nd ed. New York: Palgrave Macmillan.

Walsh, Catherine. 2009. "Estado Plurinacional e Intercultural Complementariedad y Complicidad hacia el 'Buen Vivir.' " In *Plurinacionalidad: Democracia en la Diversidad*, edited by Alberto Acosta and Esperanza Martínez, 161–84. Quito: Ediciones Abya-Yala.

Weber, Barret. 2014. " 'Government Closer to the People': On Decentralization in Nunavut." *Polar Geography* 37 (2): 177–92.

White, Graham. 1999. "Nunavut: Challenges and Opportunities of Creating a New Government." *Public Sector Management* 9 (3): 4–8.

———. 2001. "And Now for Something Completely Northern: Institutions of Governance in the Territorial North." *Journal of Canadian Studies* 35 (4): 80–99.

———. 2006. "Traditional Aboriginal Values in a Westminster Parliament: The Legislative Assembly of Nunavut." *Journal of Legislative Studies* 12 (1): 8–31.

———. 2008. " 'Not the Almighty': Evaluating Aboriginal Influence in Northern Land-Claim Boards." *Arctic* 61 (1): 71–85.

———. 2009. "Nunavut and the Inuvialuit Settlement Region: Differing Models of Northern Governance." In *Northern Exposure: Peoples, Powers, and Prospects in Canada's North*, edited by Frances Abele, Thomas J. Courchene, F. Leslie Seidle, and France St. Hilaire, 283–316. Montreal: Institute for Research on Public Policy.

———. 2013a. "In the Presence of Northern Aboriginal Women? Women in Territorial Politics." In *Stalled: The Representation of Women in Canadian Governments*, edited by Linda Trimble, Jane Arscott, and Manon Tremblay, 233–52. Vancouver: UBC Press.

———. 2013b. "Nunavut (Canada): Size Matters but So Does Culture." In *Legislatures of Small States: A Comparative Study*, edited by Nicolas D. J. Baldwin, 148–57. New York: Routledge.

———. 2020. *Indigenous Empowerment through Co-management: Land Claims Boards, Wildlife Management, and Environmental Regulation*. Vancouver: UBC Press.

Wildcat, Matthew, Mandee McDonald, Stephanie Irlbacher-Fox, and Glen Coulthard. 2014. "Learning from the Land: Indigenous Land Based Pedagogy and Decolonization." *Decolonization: Indigeneity, Education & Society* 3 (3): i–xv.

Wilson, Elana. 2005. "Gender, Nationalism, Citizenship, and Nunavut's Territorial 'House': A Case Study of the Gender Parity Proposal Debate." *Arctic Anthropology* 42 (2): 82–94.

Wolfe, Patrick. 1999. *Settler Colonialism and the Transformation of Anthropology*. London: Cassell.

Wolff, Jonas. 2012. "New Constitutions and the Transformation of Democracy in Bolivia and Ecuador." In *New Constitutionalism in Latin America: Promises and Practices*, edited by Detlef Nolte and Almut Schilling-Vacaflor, 183–202. Burlington, VT: Ashgate.

Yashar, Deborah J. 1999. "Democracy, Indigenous Movements, and the Postliberal Challenge in Latin America." *World Politics* 52 (1): 76–104.

———. 2005. *Contesting Citizenship in Latin America: The Rise of Indigenous Movements and the Postliberal Challenge*. New York: Cambridge University Press.

Younging, Gregory. 2018. *Elements of Indigenous Style: A Guide for Writing By and About Indigenous Peoples*. Edmonton: Brush Education.

Zamora Acosta, Giannina Elizabeth. 2016. "La Gestión del Territorio en un Estado Plurinacional: Retos de la Implementación del las Circunscripciones Territoriales Indígenas, como Regímenes Especiales en el Ecuador." Master's thesis, Facultad Latinoamericana de Ciencias Sociales—Ecuador.

Zamosc, Leon. 1994. "Agrarian Protest and the Indian Movement in the Ecuadorian Highlands." *Latin American Research Review* 29 (3): 37–68.

Zegada, María Teresa, Claudia Arce, Gabriela Canedo, and Alber Quispe. 2011. *La Democracia desde los Márgenes: Transformación en el Campo Político Boliviano*. La Paz: Muela del Diablo/CLACSO.

Zegada, María Teresa, and Erika Brockmann Quiroga. 2016. "Autonomías Departamentales en Bolivia: Hacia la Consolidación de un Sistema Político Multinivel." *Revista Uruguaya de Ciencia Política* 25 (1): 110–30.

# Index

## A

Acción Democrática Nacionalista (ADN), 56
activism, 20, 95, 108, 110
Afro-descendants, 10
agency, 2, 22, 32–33, 57, 104
agrarian reform, 12
Alaska, 39, 74
Amagoalik, John, 71, 73, 76–77, 84
Arctic, 17, 39, 72–74, 76, 81, 83–84
Assembly of First Nations, 8
Autonomía Indígena Originaria Campesina
  (AIOC), 64
autonomies, 23, 25, 53–55, 62, 64, 97
autonomy, 31, 37, 71, 93, 104, 108, 111;
  definition, 22; degrees, 19–20, 22–23,
  91, 105–106; demands, 2, 72, 97, 104,
  106; economic, 85; Indigenous 1, 9, 13,
  17–20, 22, 24, 26–27, 32, 34–35, 37–38,
  41, 51–52, 54–55, 58, 63–66, 68–69,
  72, 81, 87–89, 94, 97, 101–107, 109–112;
  political, 4, 25, 42, 49, 67, 73, 85; statutes
  64; territorial, 35, 101
Aymara, 53, 55, 66

## B

band council, 5, 7
bands, 17
Bolivia, 1–2, 10, 13–16, 19–20, 22–24, 26,
  30, 34–35, 53–55, 58–59, 62, 66–69,
  101, 103–108; Afro-Bolivians, 60–61;
  Anti-racism and Anti-discrimination
  Law, 63; communitarian democracy, 18,
  20, 27, 58, 60–61, 64; constitution, 13,
  18, 53–54, 58, 64–65; Framework Law
  of Autonomy and Decentralization, 25,
  64; intercultural democracy, 18, 54–55,
  61–62, 65, 68; Language Rights Law, 63;
  Law of Prior Consultation, 67; majority
  Indigenous nations, 10, 14, 53, 55, 60–61,
  64; minority Indigenous nations, 55, 60;
  National Development Plan, 66; National
  Revolution, 55; New Economic Policy,
  56; Plurinational Legislative Assembly,
  55, 60; Plurinational State, 18, 54, 59,
  61–63, 65; Transitory Electoral Regime
  Law, 60; Unity Pact, 58–59
Buen Vivir. *See* Living Well

## C

Canada, 1–9, 11, 14, 16–23, 30, 34–35, 39–44,
  46, 71–74, 76–77, 79, 82, 84–85, 107,
  109–112; British North America Act,
  6; Calder decision, 9, 40; Constitution
  Act, 6, 9, 42, 75; Department of Indian
  Affairs, 8; extinguishment clause, 7, 43;
  Indian Act, 6, 8; Royal Proclamation, 6;
  White Paper, 8
Cárdenas, Félix, 1, 26, 68
central Andes, 3, 21–22, 30, 107–108, 112
Charagua Iyambae, 64–65
Chile, 11
Circunscripción Territorial Indígena (CTI),
  89, 96, 106
Citizens' Revolution, 92
citizenship, 17, 22, 27, 31–33, 57, 107
civil servants, 63
civil society, 2, 21–22, 28–29, 33–34, 56, 58,
  91, 99, 108
coca growers, 53
Código Orgánico de Organización Territorial,
  Autonomía y Descentralización
  (COOTAD), 96–97
collective action, 27, 33, 90
colonialism, 4–5, 27, 29, 103–104. *See also*
  settler colonialism
co-management, 18, 30, 46–47, 82, 95, 104
communal justice, 30
comparative method, 3
comparative politics, 1–3
comprehensive land claims, 9, 16–17, 19, 27,
  38, 40, 42, 46, 51, 72–74, 82, 84, 105
Confederación de Nacionalidades Indígenas
  del Ecuador (CONAIE), 88–91, 93,
  99–102
Congress of Aboriginal Peoples, 8
conquistador, 10
Consejo de Desarrollo de las Nacionalidades y
  Pueblos del Ecuador (CODENPE), 95

constituent assembly, 58, 93–94
constitutional reform, 13, 20, 34, 53, 106
consultation, 29–30, 40, 49–50, 65, 67, 77, 80, 97, 99–100
co-optation, 33
corporatism, 11–13
corporatist, 12, 33
Correa, Rafael, 20, 88–89, 92–95, 98–99, 101–102, 106
Council of Yukon First Nations (CYFN), 17, 37, 50
Council for Yukon Indians (CYI), 41–43, 49, 51
courts, 8–9, 30, 40
criollo, 11
Curley, Tagak, 74, 79

**D**

debt crisis, 12, 91
decentralization, 24, 64, 80–81, 91
decolonization, 2, 14, 16, 27, 29, 55, 58, 62–63, 68, 78, 93, 104, 107; definition, 23
deepening democracy, 3, 27
democracy, 1–3, 14, 18, 20, 22, 27–33, 37–38, 54, 56, 58, 62, 65, 68, 78, 85, 89, 91–93, 104, 107–108, 110–112; pacted, 55, 57–59
democratic decolonization, 2–3, 14, 16, 22, 27–29, 33, 103–104, 107; definition 26
democratic innovation, 2, 18, 20, 27, 30, 32, 34, 46, 54–55, 65, 67–68, 82, 93, 102, 104, 108
de-patriarchalization, 62
development, 8, 12–13, 19, 35, 39, 46, 48, 66, 74, 89, 93–94, 98; economic, 4–5, 7, 58, 64–65, 73, 81–84, 95, 97, 99, 102–103, 111; political, 3, 31, 54, 57, 75, 81, 83–84, 107
devolution, 13, 40, 84
Dirección Nacional de Educación Intercultural Bilingüe (DINEIB), 95

**E**

Ecuador, 1–2, 10, 13–16, 19–20, 22–24, 26, 30, 34–35, 87–89, 91, 95, 99, 101–108, 112; constitution, 13, 19, 26, 93–94, 96–97; Environmental Action, 95; Mining Law, 95; National Indigenous Uprising, 87, 89–90; National Plan for Living Well, 94
Ecuador Runacunapac Riccharimui (ECUARUNARI), 87, 90, 101
elections, 5, 7, 17–18, 27, 30, 44, 53–54, 56–57, 59, 61, 78, 90–92, 96, 100–102, 106, 109
electoral politics, 25, 56–57, 59, 61, 77, 88, 90–91, 102, 106, 108–109

Elias, Darius, 50
elites, 11, 33, 35, 55–56, 66–67, 101
employment, 18
encomienda system, 10
extractive activities, 4, 46, 83–84, 98, 110
extractive industry, 30, 67, 73, 81–83, 88, 95, 110–111

**F**

First Nation Final Agreement (FNFA), 24, 44–45, 48
First Nations, 6–7, 17, 20, 24, 37–39, 41–52, 104–105, 109
free, prior, and informed consent (FPIC), 29–30
free-entry tenure, 39–40, 45

**G**

Gas War, 58
gender parity, 60, 77–79
governance, 4, 17–18, 20, 22, 30–34, 40, 46–47, 50, 54, 61, 65, 68, 75, 79, 82, 96, 102–104, 108; definition 29; resource, 82, 88; society-centered, 22, 30, 107. See also Indigenous governance
governance innovations. See democratic innovations
government, 1, 5–9, 12–20, 22–26, 29–30, 32, 35, 37–38, 40–44, 46–48, 50–52, 54–57, 59–68, 71–85, 88, 91, 93–96, 98–100, 102, 104–105, 108, 112

**H**

hacienda, 10, 87
High Arctic exiles, 73. See also Arctic

**I**

import-substitution industrialization (ISI), 12
Indigenous autonomy. See autonomy
Indigenous governance, 14, 21, 23, 27, 30–32, 34–35, 49, 54–55, 62, 68, 72
Indigenous identity, 6, 12, 90; status, 6, 8, 10, 12
Indigenous languages, 8, 17–18, 26, 63, 71, 78–80, 108
Indigenous law, 26, 30–31, 110
Indigenous movements, 14–16, 19, 21–22, 34, 40, 55, 58, 68, 87–88, 90–93, 95–97, 100–104, 106–108, 111–112
Indigenous nationalism, 109–110
Indigenous participation, 18, 21, 23, 27, 46, 54, 68, 82

Indigenous politics, 2–3, 5, 8, 14–15, 20, 68, 102, 107–108, 110–112
Indigenous research methods, 15
Indigenous rights, 2, 4, 7–8, 13, 18, 30–31, 34–35, 37–38, 46, 54–55, 62, 65, 67–68, 72–73, 81–82, 85, 87–89, 98–102, 104, 109–110, 112
Indigenous self-determination, 1, 4, 14–15, 20–23, 26–27, 34–35, 65, 68, 72, 74, 76, 84–85, 97–98, 103–106, 111
Indigenous self-government, 1–2, 9, 17, 19–26, 32, 34–35, 37, 39, 41–44, 46, 49, 51–52, 54–55, 65, 68–69, 72, 75–76, 81, 84–85, 87–89, 91, 96–97, 101–107, 109–112
Indigenous sovereignty, 9, 11, 13, 23, 35, 82, 87, 110
Indigenous studies, 1, 5, 15
Indigenous title, 9, 25, 40, 45, 82
Indigenous women, 111. *See also* women
Indigenous-state relations, 1–2, 5–6, 8, 11, 13, 16, 18, 24, 35, 38, 46, 48, 52, 64, 72–73, 96, 101, 103, 112
institutional arrangement, 4, 27, 30, 38, 68, 85, 105, 107
institutional participation, 22, 34, 108
institutions, 2–3, 5, 11–12, 14–15, 20–23, 25–26, 28, 34, 37, 46, 48, 54, 57–58, 61–64, 68–69, 71–72, 78–79, 82, 85, 104–106, 108–110, 112
interest representation, 12, 37, 51. *See also* representation
inter-Indigenous conflict, 90
International Labour Organization (ILO), 30, 97
International Monetary Fund (IMF), 100
Inuit, 6, 17–18, 20, 25–26, 71–85, 105–106, 109
Inuit Impact and Benefit Agreement (IIBA), 83
Inuit Owned Land (IOL), 75
Inuit Qaujimajatuqangit (IQ), 73, 79–80
Inuit Tapiriiksat Kanatami (ITK), 8
Inuit Tapirisat of Canada (ITC), 74–75

**J**
jurisdiction, 17, 22, 26, 40, 47, 64, 79, 81–83, 88, 108

**K**
Kichwa, 19, 89, 94
Kitikmeot Inuit Association, 77
Kivalliq Inuit Association, 77
Klondike Gold Rush, 38

**L**
labour, 9–10, 55–56
land, 2, 4, 7, 10–12, 17–18, 20, 22–27, 29–30, 33, 35, 38–51, 55, 71, 73–75, 81–85, 97, 105, 109, 111. *See also* settlement land
land-based politics, 2, 110
Latin America, 1–5, 7, 9–17, 19, 21–23, 29–31, 33–35, 55–56, 68, 87, 89–90, 95, 97, 99, 107, 109–112
law, 9–10, 16–17, 24, 30–31, 39–40, 48, 54, 63, 96, 98. *See also* Indigenous law
legal pluralism, 23
legislature, 18, 26, 30, 59–60, 63, 77–78, 91
Ley de Participación Popular (LPP), 24, 57
liberal, 3, 14, 19, 21, 27, 29–30, 32, 48, 59, 64–65, 68, 72, 97, 104, 107
Living Well, 19, 66, 94–95, 102

**M**
market reform, 12, 56, 90. *See also* neoliberal
Massie, Ruth, 37, 50
mestizo, 10, 12, 67
Métis, 6, 109
Métis National Council, 8
Mike, Shuvinai, 79–80
mobilization, 1, 8–10, 12, 19, 38, 57–58, 67–68, 88–90, 92, 102, 106, 111–112
Morales, Evo, 18, 20, 24–25, 53, 55, 57–60, 62–63, 65, 67–68, 106, 111
Moreno, Lenín, 99–100
Movement Toward Socialism (MAS), 18, 25, 53–55, 57–61, 63, 65–68, 106
Movimiento de la Izquierda Revolucionaria (MIR), 56
Movimiento de Unidad Plurinacional Pachakutik (MUPP), 1, 88, 90–93, 101–102, 106
Movimiento Nacional Revolucionaria (MNR), 56–57
multiculturalism, 31. *See also* neoliberal multiculturalism

**N**
nation-to-nation relations, 9, 13, 16, 19, 23–24, 30, 37, 51, 104–105, 109, 112
Native Women's Association of Canada (NWAC), 8
natural resources, 22, 58, 64, 81–82, 84, 99, 105, 110. *See also* subsurface resources
Nature, 19, 66, 88, 94, 102, 107
neoliberal, 5, 11–13, 18, 33–34, 56–58, 67, 90–92, 106
neoliberal multiculturalism, 11–13, 24
New Democratic Party (NDP), 43–44

northern Canada, 3, 21–23, 30–31, 81, 107–109
Northwest Territories (NWT), 73–74, 80, 84
Nunavut, 1–2, 13–18, 20, 22, 24–25, 30, 34,
    39, 50, 71–85, 103–107, 112; legislative
    assembly, 1, 17, 77–78; mineral rights,
    25, 75, 83; Nunavut Act, 75; Nunavut
    Leadership Forum, 78; Nunavut
    Political Accord, 75; Nunavut Wildlife
    Management Board, 18, 82–83; social
    issues, 84
Nunavut Implementation Commission (NIC),
    17–18, 71, 77
Nunavut Land Claims Agreement (NLCA), 17,
    25–26, 73–77, 82–83
Nunavut Tunngavik Incorporated (NTI),
    74–76

O

Official Languages Act, 79

P

Pachakutik. See Movimiento de Unidad
    Plurinacional Pachakutik (MUPP)
participation, 12, 18, 20–23, 25, 27–28, 30,
    33–34, 42, 46, 54, 56–58, 60, 68–69, 71,
    77, 82, 90, 93, 96, 98, 101, 103, 107–109,
    112
party politics, 15, 38, 50–51, 102, 112
Penikett, Tony, 43
Penner, Keith, 43
Pérez, Yaku, 101
plebiscite, 74, 79. See also referendum
plurinational constitutionalism, 11, 26
plurinational state, 1, 13, 18–19, 54, 59, 61–63,
    65, 87–88, 91, 93–94, 101
plurinationality, 13, 16, 20, 23, 54–55, 58,
    87–88, 91, 93–94, 101, 106, 112
political party, 1, 18, 25, 43, 50, 53–56, 59, 68,
    90–93, 101–102, 106
political will, 20, 32, 35, 88, 101
power, 3, 10–14, 27, 20–24, 28–31, 34, 37–38,
    40, 43, 47–50, 52, 54, 56–57, 61, 64–67,
    72, 81, 84, 87, 91–93, 95–97, 100, 102,
    104–107, 110, 112
prior consultation, 29, 65, 67, 97. See also free,
    prior, and informed consent (FPIC)
protest, 12, 34, 55–56, 58, 68, 90–91, 95,
    101–102, 108, 111
public policy, 33, 62, 79
public service, 40, 63, 79

Q

Qikiqtani Inuit Association, 77
Quartz Mining Act, 39
Quechua, 53, 55, 60, 66

R

referendum, 64, 96, 99–100, 109
repartimiento system, 10
representation, 2, 4, 13, 15, 18, 20, 26, 28–29,
    33, 49–50, 54, 60–62, 68–69, 72, 77, 85,
    89, 94, 101, 104, 112
reserved seats, 55, 60, 108
reserves, 6,7, 11, 76, 105
residential school, 7–9, 73
resource conflict, 55, 65
resource royalties, 46
resurgence, 2, 106
rights, 6–10, 12–13, 17–19, 22, 25–26, 32–33,
    35, 39–40, 43, 45–46, 48–49, 51–52, 63,
    65–66, 73–75, 77, 81, 83, 88, 94, 96–97,
    101–102, 107–108, 110–111. See also
    Indigenous rights
Royal Commission on Aboriginal Peoples
    (RCAP), 9

S

Sánchez de Lozada, Gonzalo, 57–58
self-determination. See Indigenous self-
    determination
self-governing First Nations, 7, 17, 38, 44,
    48–50
self-government. See Indigenous self-
    government
Self-Government Agreement (SGA), 16–17, 19,
    24, 27, 38, 47, 50
settlement land, 17, 24, 40, 44–47
settler colonialism, 4–5, 29, 103
settler state, 1, 3, 5, 7, 14, 21, 27, 107, 109, 112
Simon, Mary, 77
Smith, Elijah, 40–41
social movements, 19, 62–63, 91–92, 96, 99.
    See also Indigenous movements
sovereignty, 6, 23–24, 72–73, 82, 94. See also
    Indigenous sovereignty
structural adjustment, 56, 90. See also market
    reform
subsurface resources, 17, 24–26, 35, 39–40, 44.
    46, 51–52, 55, 73, 75, 83, 97, 110
Suma Qamaña, 66. See also Living Well
Sumac Kawsay, 19, 66. See also Living Well

## T

Territorio Indígena y Parque Nacional
  Isiboro-Sécure (TIPNIS), 66–67
territory, 11, 17, 20, 24, 26, 29, 37–40, 42,
  45–48, 51, 64, 71–72, 74–77, 80–85, 89,
  96, 106
treaty, 6, 8–9, 44, 75, 77
treaty-based relations, 7, 11, 16, 106
Truth and Reconciliation Commission (TRC),
  7
Tunngavik Federation of Nunavut (TFN),
  73–74, 76

## U

Umbrella Final Agreement (UFA), 17, 24,
  37–38, 44, 46–50
United Nations Declaration on the Rights of
  Indigenous Peoples (UNDRIP), 30, 53,
  97
United Nations Development Program
  (UNDP), 98

## V

Villa Tunari-San Ignacio de Moxos highway,
  66
violence, 66, 111

## W

Water War, 57
women, 6, 10, 32, 62–63, 77–78, 89, 111

## Y

Yasuní Ishpingo-Tambococha-Tiputin
  (Yasuní-ITT), 89, 98–99, 102
Yasunidos, 99
Yukon, 2, 13–15, 17, 19–20, 22, 24, 30, 34,
  37–52, 103–105, 107–108, 112; co-
  management boards, 46–47; legislative
  assembly, 1, 50, 52; Minto Mine, 46;
  Yukon Act, 39; Yukon Devolution
  Transfer Agreement, 40, 84; Yukon
  Forum, 24, 48

## Z

Zapatistas, 109

9 781773 855646